William Brisbane Dick

Dick's Irish dialect recitations

William Brisbane Dick

Dick's Irish dialect recitations

ISBN/EAN: 9783337126049

Printed in Europe, USA, Canada, Australia, Japan

Cover: Foto ©Andreas Hilbeck / pixelio.de

More available books at **www.hansebooks.com**

IRISH DIALECT RECITATIONS.

CONTAINING

A COLLECTION OF RARE IRISH STORIES, POETICAL AND PROSE
RECITATIONS, HUMOROUS LETTERS, IRISH WITTICISMS,
AND FUNNY RECITALS IN THE IRISH DIALECT.

EDITED BY WM. B. DICK.

NEW YORK:
DICK & FITZGERALD, PUBLISHERS,
No. 18 ANN STREET.

CONTENTS.

4   CONTENTS.

DICK'S

IRISH DIALECT RECITATIONS.

FATHER PHIL'S COLLECTION.

SAMUEL LOVER.

Abridged for Public Reading.

Father Blake was more familiarly known by the name of Father Phil. By either title, or in whatever capacity, the worthy Father had great influence over his parish, and there was a free-and-easy way with him, even in doing the most solemn duties, which agreed wonderfully with the devil-may-care spirit of Paddy. Stiff and starched formality in any way is repugnant to the very nature of Irishmen. There are forms, it is true, and many in the Romish Church, but they are not *cold* forms, but *attractive* rather, to a sensitive people; besides, I believe those very forms, when observed the least formally, are the most influential on the Irish.

With all his intrinsic worth, Father Phil was, at the same time, a strange man in exterior manners; for with an abundance of real piety, he had an abruptness of delivery, and a strange way of mixing up an occasional remark to his congregation in the midst of the celebration of the mass, which might well startle a stranger; but this very want of formality made him beloved by the people, and they would do ten times as much for Father Phil as for the severe Father Dominick.

On the Sunday in question Father Phil intended deliver-
ing an address to his flock from the altar, urging them to
the necessity of bestirring themselves in the repairs of the
chapel, which was in a very dilapidated condition, and at
one end let in the rain through its worn-out thatch. A
subscription was necessary ; and to raise this among a very
impoverished people was no easy matter. The weather
happened to be unfavorable, which was most favorable to
Father Phil's purpose, for the rain dropped its arguments
through the roof upon the kneeling people below, in the
most convincing manner ; and as they endeavored to get
out of the wet, they pressed round the altar as much as
they could, for which they were reproved very smartly by
his Reverence in the very midst of the mass. These inter-
ruptions occurred sometimes in the most serious places,
producing a ludicrous effect, of which the worthy Father
was quite unconscious, in his great anxiety to make the
people repair the chapel.

A big woman was elbowing her way towards the rails of
the altar, and Father Phil, casting a sidelong glance at
her, sent her to the right-about, while he interrupted his
appeal to Heaven to address her thus :

" *Agnus Dei*— You'd betther jump over the rails of the
althar, I think. Go along out o' that, there's plenty o'
room in the chapel below there—"

Then he would turn to the altar and proceed with the
service, till, turning again to the congregation, he perceived some fresh offender.

" *Orate, fratres!*— Will you mind what I say to you,
and go along out o' that ? There's room below there.
Thrue 'for you, Mrs. Finn—it's a shame for him to be
thramplin' on you. Go along, Darby Casey, down there,
and kneel in the rain—it's a pity you haven't a decent
woman's cloak under you, indeed ! *Orate, fratres!*"

* * * * * * *

Again he turned to pray, and after some time he made

an interval in the service to address his congregation on
the subject of the repairs, and produced a paper containing the names of subscribers to that pious work who had
already contributed, by way of example to those who had
not.

"Here it is," said Father Phil—"here it is, and no deny-
ing it—down in black and white; but if they who give are
down in black, how much blacker are those who have not
given at all! But I hope they will be ashamed of themselves when I howld up those to honor who have conthrib-
uted to the uphowlding of the house of God. And isn't it
ashamed o' yourselves you ought to be, to lave His house
in such a condition? and doesn't it rain a'most every Sunday, as if He wished to remind you of your duty? aren't
you wet to the skin a'most every Sunday? Oh, God is
good to you! to put you in mind of your duty, giving you
such bitther cowlds that you are coughing and sneezin'
every Sunday to that degree that you can't hear the blessed
mass for a comfort and a benefit to you; and so you'll go
on sneezin' until you put a good thatch on the place, and
prevent the appearance of the evidence from Heaven
against you every Sunday, which is condemning you before
your faces, and behind your backs too, for don't I see this
minute a strame o' wather that might turn a mill running
down Micky Mackavoy's back, between the collar of his
coat and his shirt?"

Here a laugh ensued at the expense of Micky Mackavoy,
who certainly *was* under a very heavy drip from the imperfect roof.

"And is it laughin' you are, you haythens?" said Father
Phil, reproving the merriment which he himself had pur-
posely created, *that he might reprove it.* "Laughin' is it
you are, at your backslidings and insensibility to the honor
of God—laughin' because when you come here to be saved,
you are lost entirely with the wet; and how, I ask you,
are my words of comfort to enter your hearts when the

rain is pouring down your backs at the same time? Sure
I have no chance of turning your hearts while you are
undher rain that might turn a mill—but once put a good
roof on the house, and I will inundate you with piety!
Maybe it's Father Dominick you would like to have coming among you, who would grind your hearts to powdher
with his heavy words." (Here a low murmur of dissent
ran through the throng.) "Ha, ha! so you wouldn't like
it, I see—very well, very well—take care, then, for if I find
you insensible to my moderate reproofs, you hard-hearted
haythens, you malefacthors and cruel persecuthors, that
won't put your hands in your pockets because your mild
and quiet poor fool of a pasthor has no tongue in his head!
I say, your mild, quiet poor fool of a pasthor (for I know
my own faults partly, God forgive me!) and I can't spake
to you as you deserve, you hard-living vagabonds, that are
as insensible to your duties as you are to the weather. I
wish it was sugar or salt that you were made of, and then
the rain might melt you if *I* couldn't; but no, them naked
rafthers grins in your face to no purpose—you chate the
house of God—but take care, maybe you won't chate
the divil so aisy." (Here there was a sensation.) "Ha,
ha! that makes you open your ears, does it? More shame
for you; you ought to despise that dirty enemy of man,
and depend on something better—but I see I must call you
to a sense of your situation with the bottomless pit undher
you, and no roof over you. Oh, dear! dear! dear! I'm
ashamed of you—throth, if I had time and sthraw enough,
I'd rather thatch the place myself than lose my time talking to you; sure the place is more like a stable than a
chapel. Oh, think of that! the house of God to be like a
stable! for though our Redeemer was born in a stable,
that is no reason why you are to keep his house always
like one.

   " And now I will read you the list of subscribers, and it
will make you ashamed when you hear the names of several

good and worthy Protestants in the parish, and out of it,
too, who have given more than the Catholics."

* * * * * * *

SUBSCRIPTION LIST.

FOR THE REPAIRS AND ENLARGEMENT OF BALLYSLOUGHGUTTHERY CHAPEL.

PHILIP BLAKE, P. P.

Micky Hickey, £0 7s. 6d. "He might as well have
made it ten shillings; but half a loaf is betther than no
bread."

"Plaze your Reverence," says Mick, from the body of
the chapel, "sure seven and sixpence is more than the
half of ten shillings." (A laugh.)

"Oh, how witty you are! Faith, if you knew your
prayers as well as your arithmetic, it would be better for
you, Micky."

Here the Father turned the laugh against Mick.

Billy Riley, £0 3s. 4d. "Of course he means to sub-
scribe again!"

John Dwyer, £0 15s. 0d. "That's something like! I'll
be bound he's only keeping back the odd five shillings for
a brush-full o' paint for the althar; it's as black as a crow,
instead o' being white as a dove."

He then hurried over rapidly some small subscribers as
follows:

Peter Hefferman, £0 1s. 8d.

James Murphy, £0 2s. 6d.

Mat Donovan, £0 1s. 3d.

Luke Dannely, £0 3s. 0d.

Jack Quigly, £0 2s. 1d.

Pat Finnegan, £0 2s. 2d.

EDWARD O'CONNOR, Esq., £2 0s. 0d. "There's for you!
Edward O'Connor, Esq.—*a Protestant in the parish*—two
pounds."

"Long life to him!" cried a voice in the chapel.

"Amen!" said Father Phil; "I'm not ashamed to be
clerk to so good a prayer."

Nicholas Fagan, £0 2s. 6d.

Young Nicholas Fagan, £0 5c. 0d. "Young Nick is betther than ould Nick, you see."

Tim Doyle, £0 7s. 6d.

Owny Doyle, £1 0s. 0d. "Well done, Owny na Coppal
—you deserve to prosper, for you make good use of your
thrivings."

Simon Leary, £0 2s. 6d.; Bridget Murphy, £0 10s. 0d.
"You ought to be ashamed o' yourself, Simon: a lone
widow woman gives more than you."

    *   *   *   *   *   *   *

Jude Moylan, £0 5s. 0d. "Very good, Judy, the women
are behaving like gentlemen; they'll have their reward in
the next world."

Pat Finnerty, £0 8s. 4d. "I'm not sure if it is 8s. 4d.
or 3s. 4d., for the figure is blotted, but I believe it is 8s. 4d."

"It was three and fourpince I gave your Reverence,"
said Pat from the crowd.

"Well, Pat, as I said eight and fourpence, you must not
let me go back o' my word, so bring me five shillings next
week."

"Sure you wouldn't have me pay for a blot, sir?"

"Yis, I would; that's the rule of backgammon, you
know, Pat. When I hit the mark, you pay for it."

Here his Reverence turned around, as if looking for some
one, and called out, "Rafferty! Rafferty! Rafferty! Where
are you, Rafferty?"

An old gray-headed man appeared, bearing a large
plate, and Father Phil continued—

"There now, be active—I'm sending him among you,
good people, and such as cannot give as much as you
would like to be read before your neighbors, give what little you can towards the repairs, and I will continue to read
out the names by way of encouragement to you—and the
next name I see is that of Squire Egan. Long life to
him!"

SQUIRE EGAN, £5 0s. 0d. "Squire Egan—five pounds —listen to that—*a Protestant in the parish*—five pounds! Faith, the Protestants will make you ashamed of yourselves if you don't take care."

Mrs. Flanagan, £2 0s. 0d. "Not her own parish, either —a fine lady."

James Milligan of Roundtown, £1 0s. 0d. "And here I must remark that the people of Roundtown have not been backward in coming forward on this occasion. I have a long list from Roundtown—I will read it separate." He then proceeded at a great pace, jumbling the town and the pounds and the people in the most extraordinary manner: "James Milligan of Roundtown, one pound; Darby Daly of Roundtown, one pound; Sam Finnegan of Roundtown, one pound; James Casey of Roundpound, one town; Kit Dwyer of Townpound, one round—pound, I mane; Pat Roundpound,—Pounden, I mane—Pat Pounden a pound of Poundtown also—there's an example for you!—

"But what are you about, Rafferty? I don't like the sound of that plate of yours—you are not a good gleaner— go up first into the gallery there, where I see so many good-looking bonnets—I suppose they will give something to keep their bonnets out of the rain, for the wet will be into the gallery next Sunday if they don't. I think that is Kitty Crow I see, getting her bit of silver ready; them ribbons of yours cost a trifle, Kitty— Well, good Christians, here is more of the subscription for you."

Matthew Lavery, £0 2s. 6d. "*He* doesn't belong to Roundtown—Roundtown will be renowned in future ages for the support of the Church. Mark my words! Roundtown will prosper from this day out—Roundtown will be a rising place."

Mark Hennessy, £0 2s. 6d.; Luke Clancy, £0 2s. 6d.; John Doolin, £0 2s. 6d. "One would think they had all agreed only to give two and sixpence apiece. And they comfortable men, too! And look at their names—Mat-

thew, Mark, Luke and John—the names of the blessed
Evangelists, and only ten shillings among them. Oh, they
are apostles not worthy the name—we'll call them the poor
apostles from this out!" (Here a low laugh ran through
the chapel.) "Do you hear that, Matthew, Mark, Luke
and John? Faith! I can tell you that name will stick to
you." (Here the laugh was louder.)

A voice, when the laugh subsided, exclaimed, "I'll make
it ten shillin's, your Reverence."

"Who's that?" said Father Phil.

"Hennessy, your Reverence."

"Very well, Mark. I suppose Matthew, Luke and John
will follow your example?"

"We will, your Reverence."

"Ha! I thought you made a mistake; we'll call you now
the faithful apostles—and I think the change in your name
is better than seven and sixpence apiece to you.

"I see you in the gallery there, Rafferty. What do you
pass that well-dressed woman for? thry back—Ha! see
that, she had her money ready if you only asked her for it
—don't go by that other woman there— Oh, ho! So you
won't give anything, ma'am? You ought to be ashamed
of yourself. There is a woman with an elegant sthraw bon-
net, and she won't give a farthing. Well now, afther that,
remember—I give it from the althar, that from this day
out sthraw bonnets pay fi'penny pieces."

Thomas Durfy, Esq., £1 0s. 0d. "It's not his parish,
and he's a brave gentleman."

Miss Fanny Dawson, £1 0s. 0d. "*A Protestant out of
the parish*, and a sweet young lady, God bless her! Oh,
faith, the Protestants is shaming you!"

Dennis Fannin, £0 7s. 6d. "Very good indeed, for a
working mason."

Jemmy Riley, £0 5s. 0d. "Not bad for a hedge car-
penther."

"I gave you ten, plaze your Reverence," shouted Jemmy; "and by the same token, you may remember it was on the Nativity of the blessed Vargin, sir, I gave you the second five shillin's."

"So you did, Jemmy," cried Father Phil; "I put a little cross before it, to remind me of it; but I was in a hurry to make a sick call when you gave it to me, and forgot it afther: and indeed myself doesn't know what I did with that same five shillings."

Here a pallid woman, who was kneeling near the rails of the altar, uttered an impassioned blessing, and exclaimed, "Oh, that was the very five shillings, I'm sure, you gave to me that very day, to buy some little comforts for my poor husband, who was dying in the fever!" and the poor woman burst into loud sobs as she spoke.

A deep thrill of emotion ran through the flock as this accidental proof of their poor pastor's beneficence burst upon them; and as an affectionate murmur began to rise above the silence which that emotion produced, the burly Father Philip blushed like a girl at this publication of his charity, and even at the foot of that altar where he stood, felt something like shame in being discovered in the commission of that virtue so highly commended by the Providence to whose worship that altar was raised. He uttered a hasty "Whisht, whisht!" and waved with his outstretched hands his flock into silence.

In an instant one of those sudden changes so common to an Irish assembly, and scarcely credible to a stranger, took place. The multitude was hushed, the grotesque of the subscription list had passed away and was forgotten, and that same man and that same multitude stood in altered relations—*they* were again a reverent flock, and *he* once more a solemn pastor; the natural play of his nation's mirthful sarcasm was absorbed in a moment in the sacredness of his office, and, with a solemnity befitting the highest occasion, he placed his hands together before his breast, and, raising his eyes to Heaven, he poured forth

his sweet voice, with a tone of the deepest devotion, in
that reverential call for prayer, " *Orate, fratres!*"

The sound of a multitude gently kneeling down followed,
like the soft breaking of a quiet sea on a sandy beach;
and when Father Philip turned to the altar to pray, his
pent-up feelings found vent in tears, and while he prayed
he wept.

I believe such scenes as this are of not unfrequent occurrence in Ireland—that country so longsuffering, so much
maligned, and so little understood.

Oh, rulers of Ireland! why have you not sooner learned
to *lead* that people by love, whom all your severity has
been unable to *drive?*

HOW PAT SAVED HIS BACON.

ANON.

Early one fine morning, as Terence O'Fleary was hard
at work in his potato-garden, he was accosted by his gos-
sip, Mick Casey, who he perceived had his Sunday clothes
on.

"God's 'bud! Terry, man, what would you be afther
doing there wid them praties, an Phelim O'Loughlin's
berrin' goin' to take place? Come along, ma bochel! sure
the praties will wait."

"Och! no," sis Terry, "I must dig on this ridge for the
childer's breakfast, an' thin I'm goin' to confession to
Father O'Higgins, who holds a stashin beyont there at his
own house."

"Bother take the stashin!" sis Mick, "sure that 'ud wait
too." But Terence was not to be persuaded.

Away went Mick to the "berrin';" and Terence, having
finished "wid the praties," as he said, went down to
Father O'Higgins, where he was shown into the kitchen,
to wait his turn for confession. He had not been long
standing there, before the kitchen fire, when his attention

was attracted by a nice piece of bacon, which hung in the chimney-corner. Terry looked at it again and again, and wished the childer " had it at home wid the praties."

"Murther alive!" says he, "will I take it? Sure the priest can spare it; an' it would be a rare thrate to Judy an' the gossoons at home, to say nothin' iv myself, who hasn't tasted the likes this many's the day." Terry looked at it again, and then turned away, saying, "I won't take it—why would I, an' it not mine, but the priest's? an' I'd have the sin iv it, sure! I won't take it," replied he, "an' it's nothin' but the Ould Boy himself that's temptin' me! But sure it's no harm to feel it, any way," said he, taking it into his hand, and looking earnestly at it. "Och! it's a beauty; and why wouldn't I carry it home to Judy and the childer? An' sure it won't be a sin afther I confesses it!"

Well, into his greatcoat pocket he thrust it; and he had scarcely done so, when the maid came in and told him that it was his turn for confession.

"Murther alive! I'm kilt and ruin'd, horse and foot, now, boy, Terry; what'll I do in this quandary, at all, at all? By gannies! I must thry an' make the best of it, any how," says he to himself, and in he went.

He knelt to the priest, told his sins, and was about to receive absolution, when all at once he seemed to recollect himself, and cried out:

"Oh! stop—stop, Father O'Higgins, dear! for goodness sake, stop! I have one great big sin to tell yit; only, sir, I'm frightened to tell id, in the regard of never having done the like afore, sur, niver!"

"Come," said Father O'Higgins. "You must tell it to me."

"Why, then, your Riverince, I will tell id; but, sir, I'm ashamed like."

"Oh, never mind! tell it," said the priest.

"Why, then, your Riverince, I went out one day to a

gintleman's house, upon a little bit of business, an' he
bein' ingaged, I was showed into the kitchen to wait.
Well, sur, there I saw a beautiful bit iv bacon hanging in
the chimbly-corner. I looked at id, your Riverince, an'
my teeth began to wather. I don't know how it was, sur,
but I suppose the Divil timpted me, for I put it into my
pocket; but, if you plaize, sur, I'll give it to you," and he
put his hand into his pocket.

"Give it to me!" said Father O'Higgins; "no, certainly
not; give it back to the owner of it."

"Why, then, your Riverince, sur, I offered id to him, and
he wouldn't take id."

"Oh! he wouldn't, wouldn't he?" said the priest;
"then take it home, and eat it yourself, with your family."

"Thank your Riverince kindly!" says Terence, "an' I'll
do that same immediately, plaize God; but first and foremost, I'll have the absolution, if you plaize, sir."

Terence received absolution, and went home rejoicing
that he had been able to save his soul and his bacon at the
same time.

PAUDEEN O'RAFFERTY'S SAY VOYAGE.

ANONYMOUS.

A Laughable Irish Recitation.

Sure now, ladies and gintlemen, if ye plaze, I'll relate
the great mistake I made when I came here to Naples—
stop, aisy, Paudeen, and don't decaive the ladies and gintlemen; for, bedad, I didn't come at all; they brought
me, in a ship—a grate big ship, with two big sticks standing out of it. Masts they call them, bad luck to it and the
day I saw it. If I had been an ignorant fellow and didn't
know joggraphy and the likes, I'd be safe enough at home
now, so I would, in me own cellar, on the Coal-Quay in

Dublin. But, divil fire. me! I must be making a man of myself, showing me larnin', me knowledge of similitude, and the likes. You see, I wint over to England on a bit of an agricultural speculation—hay-makin' and harvest-rapin'—and, the saison bein' good, I realized a fortune, so I did—a matter of thirty shillings or so.

So says I to myself, says I, "Now I have got an indipindant competance, I'll go back to Ireland—I ll buy it out, and make meself emperor of it." So I axed one of the boys which was my nearest way to Bristol, to go be the say. So, says one of them—(be the same token he was a cousin of mine—one Terry O'Rafferty—as dacint a boy as you could wish to meet, and as handy with a shillaly. Why, I ve seen him clear a tint at Donnybrook fair in less than two minutes, with divil a won to help except his bit of a stick, an' you know that's no aisy job.)

Well, says Terry to me, says he, "Go down to the quay," says he, "and you'll find out all about it while a cat 'd be lickin' her ear."

Well, I wint to a man that was standin' by the dure of a public house—it was the sign of—the sign——What the divil is this the sign was?—you see I like to be sarcum-spectious in me joggraphy—it was the sign of the blind cow kicking the dead man's eyes out—or the dead man kicking the blind cows eyes out—or the dead man's cow kicking the blind—no—well, it was something that way, anyhow.

So says I to the man, "Sir," says I, "I want a ship."

"There you are," says he.

"Where?" says I.

"There," says he.

"Thank you," Says I. "Which of thim's for Ireland?"

"Oh, you're an ould-countryman," says he.

"How the divil did you find that out?" says I.

"I know it," says he.

"Who tould you?" says I.

"No matther," says he. "Come," says he.

"I will," says I.

Well, we wint in, and we had a half a pint of whisky. Oh, bedad, it 'd have done your heart good to see the bade rise on the top of it. Maybe my heart didn't warm to him, an' his to me, aw murther!

"Erin go bragh!" says he.

"Ceadh mille failthe!" says I.

And there we wor, like two sons of an Irish king, in less than a minute.

Thin we got to discoorsing about Dublin and Naples, an' other furrin parts that we wor acquainted with, and he began talking about how like the Bay of Naples was to the Bay of Dublin—for, you see, he was an ould soger, d'ye mind?—an' thim ould sogers are always mighty 'cute chaps. He was a grate big chap that was off in the wars among the Frinch and the Spaniards and the Rushers, and other barbarians. So we got talking of similitude an' joggraphy, an' the likes, and mixin' Naples an' wather and Dublin an' whisky; and be me sowl, purty punch we made of it!

I was in the middle o' my glory, whin in walks the captain o' the ship.

"Any one here to go aboord?" says he.

"Here I am," says I.

And be the same token, me head was quite soft with the whisky, and talking about Dublin an' Naples, and Naples an' whisky, and wather an' Dublin, Dublin an' Naples, Naples an' Dublin—bad cess to me! but I said the one place instead of the other, whin they axed me where I was going, d'ye mind?

Well, they brought me aboord the ship as dhrunk as a lord, and threw me down in the cellar—the hould, they called it, and the divil's own hould it was—wid sacks, pigs, praties, an' other passengers, an' there they left me in lavendher, like Paddy Ward's pig.

I fell asleep the first week. Whin I woke up, didn't I heave ahead in me sthomatics enough to make me backbone an' me ribs strike fire!

"Arrah," says I to meself, says I, "are they ever going to take me home?"

Just thin I h'ard a voice sing out:

"There's the Bay!"

That was enough for me. I scrambled up-stairs till I got on the roof—the deck they call it—as fast as me legs could carry me.

"Land-ho!" says one of the chaps.

"Where?" says I.

"There it is," says he.

"For the love of glory, show me where!" says I.

"There, over the cat's head," says he.

I looked around, but the divil recaive the cat's-head or dog's tail aither I could see! The blaggard stared at me as if I was a banshee or a fairy. I gev another look, and there was the Bay, sure enough, afore me.

"Arrah good luck to you!" says I, "but you warm the cockles of me heart. But what's come over the Hill of Howth?" says I. "It used to be a civil, paiceable soort of a mountain; but now it's splutthering an' smokin' away like a grate big lime-kiln. Sure the boys must have lit a big bone-fire on top of it, to welcome me!"

With that, a vagabone that was listenin' to me, cries out in a horse-laugh:

"Hill of Howth?" says he. "You're a Grecian—that's not the Hill of Howth."

"Not the Hill of Howth?" says I.

"No," says he. "That's Mount Vesuvius."

"Aisy, aisy!" says I. "Isn't Mount Vesulpherous in Italy?"

"Yis," says he.

"An' isn't Italy in France?" says I.

"Of coorse it is," says he.

" An' isn't France in Gibberalther ?" says I.

" To be sure," says he.

" An' isn't Gibberalther in Russia ?" says I.

" Maybe so," says he.   " But we're in Italy, anyhow—
this is the Bay of Naples, and that is Mount Vesuvius."

" Are you sure ?" says I.

" I am," says he.

And, be me sowl, it was thrue for him.   *The ship made
a big blundher* in takin' me to Naples, whin I wanted to
go to Dublin, d'ye mind ?

HANDY ANDY'S LITTLE MISTAKES.

LOVER.

A Laughable Irish Story.

Andy Rooney was a fellow who had the most singularly
ingenious knack of doing everything the wrong way; dis-
appointment waited on all affairs in which he bore a part,
and destruction was at his fingers' ends: so the nickname
the neighbors stuck upon him was Handy Andy, and the
jeering jingle pleased him.

When Andy grew up to be what in country parlance is
called " a brave lump of a boy," his mother thought he
was old enough to do something for himself; so she took
him one day along with her to the squire's, and waited
outside the door, loitering up and down the yard behind
the house, among a crowd of beggars and great lazy dogs,
that were thrusting their heads into every iron pot that
stood outside the kitchen door, until chance might give
her " a sight o' the squire afore he wint out, or afore he
wint in;" and after spending her entire day in this idle
way, at last the squire made his appearance, and Judy
presented her son, who kept scraping his foot, and pulling
his forelock, that stuck out like a piece of ragged thatch
from his forehead, making his obeisance to the squire,
while his mother was sounding his praises for being the

"handicst crayther alive—and so willin'—nothin' comes wrong to him."

"I suppose the English of all this is, you want me to take him?" said the squire.

"Throth, an' your honor, that's just it—if your honor would be plazed."

"What can he do?"

"Anything, your honor."

"That means *nothing*, I suppose," said the squire.

"Oh, no, sir. Everything, I mane, that you would desire him to do."

To every one of these assurances on his mother's part, Andy made a bow and a scrape.

"Can he take care of horses?"

"The best of care, sir," said the mother, while the miller, who was standing behind the squire, waiting for orders, made a grimace at Andy, who was obliged to cram his face into his hat to hide the laugh, which he could hardly smother from being heard, as well as seen.

"Let him come, then, and help in the stables, and we'll see what he can do."

"May the Lord—"

"That'll do—there, now go."

"Oh, sure, but I'll pray for you, and—"

"Will you go?"

"And may the angels make your honor's bed this blessed night, I pray."

"If you don't go, your son shan't come."

Judy and her hopeful boy turned to the right-about in double-quick time, and hurried down the avenue.

The next day Andy was duly installed into his office of stable-helper; and, as he was a good rider, he was soon made whipper-in to the hounds, for there was a want of such a functionary in the establishment; and Andy's boldness in this capacity soon made him a favorite with the squire, who was one of those rollicking boys on the pattern of the old school, who scorned the attentions of a regular valet, and let any one that chance threw in his way bring him his boots, or his hot water for shaving, or his coat, whenever it *was* brushed. One morning, Andy, who was very often the attendant on such occasions, came to his room with hot water. He tapped at the door.

" Who's that ?" said the squire, who had just risen, and did not know but it might be one of the women servants.

" It's me, sir."

" Oh—Andy ! Come in."

" Here's the hot water, sir," said Andy, bearing an enormous tin can.

" Why, what the devil brings that enormous tin can here ? You might as well bring the stable bucket."

" I beg your pardon, sir," said Andy, retreating. In two minutes more Andy came back, and, tapping at the door, put in his head cautiously and said, " The maids in the kitchen, your honor, says there's not so much hot water ready."

" Did I not see it a moment since in your hand ?"

" Yes, sir ; but that's not nigh the full o' the stable-bucket !"

" Go along, you stupid thief ! and get me some hot water directly."

" Will the can do, sir ?"

" Ay, anything, so you make haste."

Off posted Andy, and back he came with the can.

" Where'll I put it, sir ?"

" Throw this out," said the squire, handing Andy a jug containing some cold water, meaning the jug to be replenished with the hot.

Andy took the jug, and the window of the room being open, he very deliberately threw the jug out. The squire started with wonder, and at last said :

" What did you do that for ?"

" Sure you *towld* me to throw it out, sir."

" Go out of this, you thick-headed villain!" said the
squire, throwing his boots at Andy's head, along with some
very neat curses.   Andy retreated, and thought himself a
very ill-used person.

The first time Andy was admitted into the mysteries of
the dining-room, great was his wonder.   The butler took
him in to give him some previous instructions, and Andy
was so lost in admiration at the sight of the assembled
glass and plate, that he stood with his mouth and eyes
wide open, and scarcely heard a word that was said to
him.

" What are you looking at ?" said the butler.

" Them things, sir," said Andy, pointing to some silver
forks.

" Is it the forks ?" said the butler.

" Oh no, sir.   I know what forks is very well; but I
never seen them things afore."

" What things do you mean ?"

" These things, sir," said Andy, taking up one of the
silver forks, and turning it round and round in his hand
in utter astonishment, while the butler grinned at his
ignorance, and enjoyed his own superior knowledge.

" Well," said Andy, after a long pause, " the devil be
from me if ever I seen a silver spoon split that way before !"

The butler gave a horse-laugh, and made a standing
joke of Andy's split spoon ; but time and experience made
Andy less impressed with wonder at the show of plate and
glass, and the split spoons became familiar as " household
words " to him ; yet still there were things in the duties of
table attendance beyond Andy's comprehension—he used
to hand cold plates for fish, and hot plates for jelly, etc.
But " one day," as Zanga says—" one day " he was thrown
off his centre in a remarkable degree by a bottle of soda-
water.

It was when that combustible was first introduced into

Ireland as a dinner beverage that the occurence took
place, and Andy had the luck to be the person to whom a
gentleman applied for some soda-water.

" Sir ?" said Andy.

" Soda-water," said the guest, in that subdued tone in
which people are apt to name their wants at a dinner-table.

Andy went to the butler.

" Mr. Morgan, there's a gintleman—"

" Let me alone, will you ?" said Morgan.

Andy maneuvered round him a little longer, and again
essayed to be heard.

" Mr. Morgan !"

" Don't you see I'm as busy as I can be ?　Can't you do
it yourself ?"

" I dunno what he wants."

" Well, go and ax him," said Mr. Morgan.

Andy went off as he was bidden, and came behind the
thirsty gentleman's chair, with " I beg your pardon, sir."

" Well," said the gentleman.

" I beg your pardon, sir; but what's this you axed me
for ?"

" Soda-water."

" What, sir ?"

" Soda-water; but perhaps you have not any."

" Oh, there's plenty in the house, sir !　Would you like
it hot, sir ? "

The gentleman laughed, and supposing the new fashion
was not understood in the present company, said, " Never
mind."

But Andy was too anxious to please to be so satisfied,
and again applied to Mr. Morgan.

" Sir ! " said he.

" Bad luck to you !—can't you let me alone ? "

" There's a gentleman wants some soap and wather."

" Some what ? "

" Soap and wather, sir."

" Divil sweep you !—Soda-wather, you mano. You'll get it under the sideboard."

" Is it in the can, sir ? "

" The curse o' Crum'll on you ! in the bottles."

" Is this it, sir ?" said Andy, producing a bottle of ale.

" No, bad cess to you !—the little bottles."

" Is it the little bottles with no bottoms, sir ?"

" I wish *you* wor in the bottom o' the say !" said Mr. Morgan, who was fuming and puffing, and rubbing down his face with a napkin, as he was hurrying to all quarters of the room, or, as Andy said, in praising his activity, that he was, " like bad luck—everywhere."

" There they are !" said Morgan at last.

" Oh ! them bottles that won't stand," said Andy ; "sure them's what I said, with no bottoms to them. How'll I open it ?—it's tied down."

" Cut the cord, you fool !"

Andy did as he was desired ; and he happened at the time to hold the bottle of soda-water on a level with the candles that shed light over the festive board from a large silver branch, and the moment he made the incision, bang went the bottle of soda, knocking out two of the lights with the projected cork, which, performing its parabola the length of the room, struck the squire himself in the eye at the foot of the table ; while the hostess at the head had a cold bath down her back. Andy, when he saw the soda-water jumping out of the bottle, held it from him at arm's length ; every fizz it made, exclaiming, " Ow !—ow ! —ow !—" and, at last, when the bottle was empty, he roared out, " Oh, Lord—it's all gone !"

Great was the commotion ;—few could resist laughter except the ladies, who all looked at their gowns, not liking the mixture of satin and soda-water. The extinguished candles were re-lighted—the squire got his eye open again —and the next time he perceived the butler sufficiently near to speak to him, he said in a low and hurried tone of

deep anger, while he knit his brow, " Send that fellow out of
the room!" but, within the same instant, resumed the former smile, that beamed on all around as if nothing had
happened.

Andy was expelled the dining-room in disgrace, and
for days kept out of the master's and mistress's way : in
the meantime the butler made a good story of the thing in
the servants' hall ; and, when he held up Andy's ignorance
to ridicule, by telling how he asked for " soap and water,"
Andy was given the name of " Suds," and was called by
no other for months after.

But, though Andy's functions in the interior were suspended, his services in out-of-door affairs were occasionally
put in requisition. But here his evil genius still haunted
him, and he put his foot in a piece of business his master
sent him upon one day, which was so simple as to defy
almost the chance of Andy making any mistake about it ;
but Andy was very ingenious in his own particular line.

" Ride into the town and see if there's a letter for me,"
said the squire one day to our hero.

" Yes, sir."

" You know where to go ?"

" To the town, sir."

" But do you know where to go in the town ?"

" No, sir."

" And why don't you ask, you stupid thief ?"

" Sure I'd find out, sir."

" Didn't I often tell you to ask what you're to do, when
you don't know ?"

" Yes, sir."

" And why don't you ?"

" I don't like to be troublesome, sir."

" Confound you !" said the squire ; though he could not
help laughing at Andy's excuse for remaining in ignorance.
" Well," continued he, " go to the post-office. You know
the post-office I suppose ?"

" Yes, sir ; where they sell gunpowder."

" You're right for once," said the squire ; for his majesty's postmaster was the person who had the privilege of dealing in the aforesaid combustible.   " Go then to the post-office and ask for a letter for me.   Remember, not gunpowder, but a letter."

" Yis, sir," said Andy, who got astride of his hack, and trotted away to the post-office.   On arriving at the shop of the postmaster (for that person carried on a brisk trade in groceries, gimlets, broadcloth, and linen-drapery), Andy presented himself at the counter, and said, " I want a letther, sir, if you plaze."

" Who do you want it for ?" said the postmaster, in a tone which Andy considered an aggression upon the sacredness of private life ; so Andy thought the coolest contempt he could throw upon the prying impertinence of the postmaster was to repeat his question.

" I want a letther, sir, if you plaze."

" And who do you want it for ?" repeated the postmaster.

" What's that to you ?" said Andy.

The postmaster, laughing at his simplicity, told him he could not tell what letter to give him unless he told him the directions.

" The directions I got was to get a letther here—that's the directions."

" Who gave you those directions ?"

" The masther."

" And who's your master ?"

" What consarn is that o' yours ?"

" Why, you stupid rascal ! if you don't tell me his name, how can I give you a letter ?"

" You could give it if you liked, but you're fond of axin' impident questions, bekase you think I'm simple."

" Go along out o' this !   Your master must be as great a goose as yourself, to send such a messenger."

"Bad luck to your impidence," said Andy; "is it Squire Egan you dare to say goose to?"

"Oh, Squire Egan's your master, then?"

"Yes; have you anything to say agin it?"

"Only that I never saw you before."

"Faith, then you'll never see me agin if I have my own consent."

"I won't give you any letter for the squire, unless I know you're his servant. Is there any one in the town knows you?"

"Plenty," said Andy; "it's not every one is as ignorant as you."

Just at this moment a person to whom Andy was known entered the house, who vouched to the postmaster that he might give Andy the squire's letter. "Have you one for me?"

"Yes, sir," said the postmaster, producing one—"four-pence."

The gentleman paid the fourpence postage, and left the shop with his letter.

"Here's a letter for the squire," said the postmaster; "you've to pay me elevenpence postage."

"What 'ud I pay elevenpence for?"

"For postage."

"To the divil wid you! Didn't I see you give Mr. Durfy a letther for fourpence this minit, and a bigger letter than this? and now you want me to pay elevenpence for this scrap of a thing. Do you think I'm a fool?"

"No; but I'm sure of it," said the postmaster.

"Well, you're welkim to be sure, sure;—but don't be delayin' me now: here's fourpence for you, and gi' me the letther."

"Go along, you stupid thief!" said the postmaster, taking up the letter, and going to serve a customer with a mousetrap.

While this person and many others were served, Andy

lounged up and down the shop, every now and then putting in his head in the middle of the customers, and saying, " Will you gi' me the letther?"

He waited for above half an hour, in defiance of the anathemas of the postmaster, and at last left, when he found it impossible to get common justice for his master, which he thought he deserved as well as another man; for, under this impression, Andy determined to give no more than fourpence.

The squire in the meantime was getting impatient for his return, and when Andy made his appearance asked if there was a letter for him.

" There is, sir," said Andy.

" Then give it to me."

" I haven't it, sir."

" What do you mean?"

" He wouldn't give it to me, sir."

" Who wouldn't give it to you?"

" That owld chate beyant in the town—wanting to charge double for it."

" Maybe it's a double letter. Why the devil didn't you pay what he asked, sir?"

" Arrah, sir, why would I let you be chated? It's not a double letther at all: not above half the size o' one Mr. Durfy got before my face for fourpence."

" You'll provoke me to break your neck some day, you vagabond! Ride back for your life, you omadhaun; and pay whatever he asks, and get me the letter."

" Why, sir, I tell you he was selling them before my face for fourpence apiece."

" Go back, you scoundrel! or I'll horsewhip you; and if you're longer than an hour, I'll have you ducked in the horsepond!"

Andy vanished, and made a second visit to the post-office. When he arrived, two other persons were getting letters, and the postmaster was selecting the epistles for

each, from a large parcel that lay before him on the
counter; at the same time many shop customers were
waiting to be served.

"I'm come for the letther," said Andy.

"I'll tend to you by and by."

"The masther's in a hurry."

"Let him wait till his hurry's over."

"He'll murther me if I'm not back soon."

"I'm glad to hear it."

While the postmaster went on with such provoking
answers to these appeals for dispatch, Andy's eye caught
the heap of letters which lay on the counter: so, while
certain weighing of soap and tobacco was going forward,
he contrived to become pessessed of two letters from the
heap, and, having effected that, waited patiently enough
till it was the great man's pleasure to give him the missive
directed to his master.

Then did Andy bestride his hack, and in triumph at his
trick on the postmaster, rattle along the road homeward
as fast as the beast could carry him. He came into the
squire's presence, his face beaming with delight, and an
air of self-satisfied superiority in his manner, quite unac-
countable to his master, until he pulled forth his hand,
which had been grubbing up his prizes from the bottom of
his pocket; and holding three letters over his head, while
he said, "Look at that!" he next slapped them down under his broad fist on the table before the squire, saying:

"Well! if he did make me pay elevenpence, by gor, I
brought your honor the worth o' your money anyhow!"

JIMMY BUTLER AND THE OWL.

An Irish Story.   ANONYMOUS.

'Twas in the summer of '46 that I landed at Hamilton,
fresh as a new pratie just dug from the "ould sod," and
wid a light heart and a heavy bundle I sot off for the

township of Buford, tiding a taste of a song, as merry a young fellow as iver took the road. Well, I trudged on and on, past many a plisint place, pleasin' myself wid the thought that some day I might have a place of my own, wid a world of chickens and ducks and pigs and childer about the door; and along in the afternoon of the sicond day I got to Buford village. A cousin of me mother's, one Dennis O'Dowd, lived about sivin miles from there, and I wanted to make his place that night, so I inquired the way at the tavern, and was lucky to find a man who was goin' part of the way an' would show me the way to find Dennis. Sure he was very kind indade, an' when I got out of his wagon he pointed me through the wood and tould me to go straight south a mile an' a half, and the first house would be Dennis's.

"An' you've no time to lose now," said he, "for the sun is low, and mind you don't get lost in the woods."

"Is it lost now," said I, "that I'd be gittin, an' me uncle as great a navigator as iver steered a ship across the thrackless say! Not a bit of it, though I'm obleeged to ye for your kind advice, and thank yiz for the ride."

An' wid that he drove off an' left me alone. I shouldered me bundle bravely, an' whistlin' a bit of time for company like, I pushed into the bush. Well, I went a long way over bogs, and turnin' round among the bush an' trees till I began to think I must be well-nigh to Dennis's. But, bad cess to it! all of a sudden I came out of the woods at the very identical spot where I started in, which I knew by an' ould crotched tree that seemed to be standin' on its head an' kickin' up its heels to make divarsion of me. By this time it was growin' dark, and as there was no time to lose, I started in a second time, determined to keep straight south this time, and no mistake. I got on bravely for a while, but och hone! och hone! it got so dark I couldn't see the trees, and I bumped me nose and barked me shins, while the miskaties bit me

hands and face to a blister; an' after tumblin' and stum-
blin' around till I was fairly bamfoozled, I sat down on a
log, all of a trimble, to think that I was lost intirely, an'
that maybe a lion or some other wild craythur would de-
vour me before morning.

Just then I heard somebody a long way off say, "Whip
poor Will!" "Bedad!" sez I, "I'm glad it isn't Jamie
that's got to take it, though it seems it's more in sorrow
than in anger they are doin' it, or why should they say,
'poor Will?' an' sure they can't be Injin, haythin, or naygur, for it's plain English they're afther spakin'. Maybe
they might help me out of this," so I shouted at the top of
my voice, "A lost man!" Thin I listened. Prisently an
answer came.

"Who? Whoo? Whooo?"

"Jamie Butler, the waiver!" sez I, as loud as I could
roar, an' snatchin' up me bundle an' stick, I started in the
direction of the voice. Whin I thought I had got near
the place I stopped and shouted again. "A lost man!"

"Who! Whoo! Whooo!" said a voice right over my
head.

"Sure," thinks I, "it's a mighty quare place for a man
to be at this time of night; maybe it's some settler scrapin' sugar off a sugar bush for the children's breakfast in
the mornin'. But where's Will and the rest of them?" All
this wint through me head like a flash, an' then I answered
his inquiry.

"Jamie Butler, the waiver," sez I; "and if it wouldn't
inconvanience yer honor, would yez be kind enough to
step down and show me the way to the house of Dennis
O'Dowd?"

"Who! Who! Whooo!" sez he.

"Dennis O'Dowd!" sez I, civil enough, "and a dacent
man he is, and first cousin to me own mother."

"Who! Whoo! Whooo!" sez he again.

"Me mother!" sez I, "and as fine a woman as iver

And sounded aloud with the Irishman's bang,
The wife scream'd aloud, and the husband appears
At the window, his shoulders shrugg'd up to his ears.
" So ho! honest friend, pray what is the matter,
That at this time of night you should make such a clatter?"
" Go to bed! go to bed!" says Pat, " my dear honey
I am not a robber to ask for your money ;
I borrow'd your knocker before it was day,
To waken the landlord right over the way."

AN IRISH LETTER.

Written during the Rebellion by an Irish Member of Parliament to his friend in London.

MY DEAR SIR: Having now a little peace and quietness,
I sit down to inform you of the dreadful bustle and con-
fusion we are in from these bloodthirsty rebels, most of
whom are, I am glad to say, killed and dispersed. We are
in a pretty mess, can get nothing to eat, nor wine to drink,
except whisky, and when we sit down to dinner we are
obliged to keep both hands armed. Whilst I write this, I
hold a sword in each hand and a pistol in the other. I
concluded from the beginning that this would be the end
of it, and I see I was right, for it is not half over yet. At
present there are such goings on that everything is at a
stand-still.

I should have answered your letter a fortnight ago, but
I did not receive it till this morning. Indeed, scarcely a
mail arrives safe without being robbed. No longer ago
than yesterday the coach with the mails from Dublin was
robbed near this town ; the bags had been judiciously left
behind for fear of accident, and by good luck there was
nobody in it but two outside passengers, who had nothing
for the thieves to take.

Last Thursday notice was given that a gang of rebels
was advancing here under the French standard, but they

had no colors, nor any drums except bagpipes. Immediately every man in the place, including women and children, ran out to meet them. We soon found our force much too little; we were far too near to think of retreating. Death was in every face, but to it we went, and by the time half our little party were killed, we began to be all alive again. Fortunately the rebels had no guns, except pistols, cutlasses and pikes, and as we had plenty of muskets and ammunition, we put them all to the sword. Not a soul of them escaped, except some that were drowned in an adjacent bog, and, in a very short time, nothing was to be heard but silence. Their uniforms were all different colors, but mostly green. After the action we went to rummage a sort of camp, which they had left behind them. All we found was a few pikes without heads, a parcel of empty bottles full of water, and a bundle of French commissions filled up with Irish names. Troops are now stationed all round the country, which exactly squares with my ideas.

I have only time to add that I am in great haste.

Yours truly,

P. S.—If you do not receive this, of course it must have miscarried, therefore I beg you will write to let me know.

RORY O'MORE'S PRESENT TO THE PRIEST.

SAMUEL LOVER.

An Irish Recitation.

" Why, thin, I'll tell you," said Rory. " I promised my mother to bring a present to the priest from Dublin, and I could not make up my mind rightly what to get all the time I was there. I thought of a pair o' top-boots; for, indeed, his reverence's is none of the best, and only you *know* them to be top-boots, you would not *take* them to be

top-boots, bekase the bottoms has been put in so often
that the tops is worn out intirely, and is no more like top-
boots than my brogues. So I went to a shop in Dublin,
and picked out the purtiest pair o' top-boots I could see;
whin I say purty, I don't mane a flourishin' taarin' pair,
but sitch as was fit for a priest, a respectable pair of boots;
and with that, I pulled out my good money to pay for thim,
whin jist at that minit, remembering the thricks o' the
town, I bethought o' myself, and says I, 'I suppose these
are the right thing?' says I to the man. 'You can thry
them,' says he. 'How can I thry them?' says I. 'Pull
them on you,' says he. 'Troth, an' I'd be sorry,' said I,
'to take such a liberty with them,' says I. 'Why, aren't
you goin' to ware thim?' says he. 'Is it me?' says I, 'me
ware top-boots? Do you think it's takin' lave of me sinsis
I am?' says I. 'Then what do you want to buy them for?'
says he. 'For his reverence, Father Kinshela,' says I.
'Are they the right sort for him?' 'How should I know?'
says he. 'You're a purty bootmaker,' says I, 'not to know
how to make a priest's boot!' 'How do I know his size?'
says he. 'Oh, don't be comin' off that way,' says I. 'There's
no sitch great differ betune priests and other min!'"

"I think you were very right there," said the pale
traveler.

"To be sure, sir," said Rory; "and it was only jist a
come-off for his own ignorance. 'Tell me his size,' says
the fellow, 'and I'll fit him.' 'He's betune five and six
fut,' says I. 'Most men are,' says he, laughin' at me. He
was an impident fellow. 'It's not the five, nor the six, but
his *two* feet I want to know the size of,' says he. So I
persaived he was jeerin' me, and says I, 'Why, thin, you
respectful vagabone o' the world, you Dublin jackeen! do
you mane to insinivate that Father Kinshela ever wint bare-
futted in his life, that I could know the size of his fut?'
says I; and with that I threw the boots in his face. 'Take
that,' says I, 'you dirty thief o' the world! you impident

vagabone of the world! you ignorant citizen of the world!'
And with that I left the place."

"It is their usual practice," said the traveler, "to take
measure of their customers."

"Is it, thin?"

"It really is."

"See that, now!" said Rory, with an air of triumph.
"You would think that they wor cleverer in the town
than in the country; and they ought to be so, by all accounts; but in the regard of what I towld you, you see,
we're before them intirely."

"How so?" said the traveler.

"Arrah! bekase they never throuble people in the
country at all with takin' their measure; but you jist go to
a fair, and bring your fut along with you, and somebody
else dhrives a cartful o' brogues into the place, and there
you sarve yourself; and so the man gets his money, and
you get your shoes, and every one's plazed."

"But what I mane is, where did I leave off tellin' you
about the present for the priest? wasn't it at the bootmaker's shop? yes, that was it. Well, sir, on lavin' the
shop, as soon as I kem to myself afther the fellow's
impidence, I began to think what was the next best thing
I could get for his reverence ; and with that, while I was
thinkin' about it, I seen a very respectable owld gintleman
goin' by, with the most beautiful stick in his hand I ever
set my eyes on, and a goolden head to it that was worth
its weight in goold ; and it gev him such an illigánt look
altogether, that says I to myself, 'It's the very thing for
Father Kinshela, if I could get sitch another.' And so I
wint lookin' about me every shop I seen as I wint by, and
at last, in a sthreet they call Dame sthreet, and by the
same token I didn't know why they called it Dame sthreet
till I ax'd; and I was towld they called it Dame sthreet
bekase the ladies were so fond o' walkin' there ; and lovely
craythurs they were ! and I can't believe that the town is

such an onwholesome place to live in, for most o' the ladies
I seen there had the most beautiful rosy cheeks I ever
clapt my eyes upon ; and the beautiful rowlin' eyes o' them !
Well, it was in Dame sthreet, as I was sayin', that I kem
to a shop where there was a power o' sticks, and so I
wint in and looked at thim ; and a man in the place kem
to me and ax'd me if I wanted a cane. 'No,' says I, 'I
don't want a cane ; it's a stick I want,' says I. 'A cane,
you *mane*,' says he. 'No,' says I, 'it's a stick,' for I was
determined to have no cane, but to stick to the stick.
'Here's a nate one,' says he. 'I don't want a *nate* one,'
says I, 'but a responsible one,' says I. 'Faith !' says he,
'if an Irishman's stick was responsible, it would have a
great dale to answer for,' and he laughed a power ; I
didn't know myself what he meant, but that's what he
said."

"It was because you asked for a responsible stick," said
the traveler.

"And why wouldn't I," said Rory, "when it was for his
reverence I wanted it ? Why wouldn't he have a nice-
looking, respectable, responsible stick ?"

"Certainly," said the traveler.

"Well, I picked out one that looked to my likin', a good
substantial stick, with an ivory top to it; for I seen that
the goold-headed ones was so dear that I couldn't come up
to them; and so says I, 'Give me a howld o' that,' says I,
and I tuk a grip iv it. I never was so surprised in my life.
I thought to get a good, brave handful of a solid stick,
but, my dear, it was well it didn't fly out o' my hand
a'most, it was so light. 'Phew !' says I, 'what sort of a
stick is this ?' 'I tell you it's not a stick, but a cane,' says
he. 'Faith! I b'lieve you,' says I. 'You see how good
and light it is,' says he. Think o' that, sir! to call a stick
good and light, as if there could be any good in life in a
stick that wasn't heavy and could sthreck a good blow !
'Is it jokin' you are ?' says I. 'Don't you feel it yourself ?'

says he. 'Throth, I can hardly feel it at all,' says I. 'Sure that's the beauty of it,' says he. Think o' the ignorant vagabone! to call a stick a beauty that was as light a'most as a bulrush! 'And so you can hardly feel it!' says he, grinnin'. 'Yis, indeed,' says I; 'and what's worse, I don't think I could make any one else feel it, either.' 'Oh! you want a stick to bate people with!' says he. 'To be sure,' says I; 'sure that's the use of a stick.' 'To knock the sinsis out o' people!' says he, grinnin' again. 'Sartinly,' says I, 'if they're saucy,' lookin' hard at him at the same time. 'Well, these is only walkin'-sticks,' says he. 'Throth, you may say *runnin'*-sticks,' says I, 'for you daren't stand before any one with sitch a *thraneen* as that in your fist.' 'Well, pick out the heaviest o' them you plaze,' says he; 'take your choice.' So I wint pokin' and rummagin' among thim, and, if you believe me, there wasn't a stick in their whole shop worth a kick in the shins —divil a one!"

"But why did you require such a heavy stick for the priest?"

"Bekase there's not a man in the parish wants it more," says Rory.

"Is he so quarrelsome, then?' said the traveler.

"No, but the greatest o' pacemakers," says Rory.

"Then what does he want the heavy stick for?"

"For wallopin' his flock, to be sure," said Rory.

"Walloping!" said the traveler, choking with laughter.

"Oh! you may laugh," said Rory, "but, 'pon me sowl! you wouldn't laugh if you wor undher his hand, for he has a brave heavy one, God bless him and spare him to us!"

"And what is all this walloping for?"

"Why, sir, whin we have a bit of a fight, for fun, or the regular faction one, at the fair, his reverence sometimes hears of it, and comes av coorse!"

"Good God!" said the traveler, in real astonishment, "does the priest join in the battle?"

" No, no, no, sir! I see you're quite a sthranger in the counthry. The priest join in! Oh! by no manes. But he comes and stops it; and av coorse the only way he can stop it is to ride into thim, and wallop thim all round before him, and disparse thim; scatter thim like chaff before the wind; and it's the best o' sticks he requires for that same."

" But might he not have his heavy stick for that purpose, and make use of a lighter one on other occasions ?"

" As for that matther, sir," said Rory, " there's no knowin' the minit he might want it, for he is often necessitated to have recoorse to it. It might be, going through the village, the public-house is too full, and in he goes and dhrives thim out. Oh! it would delight your heart to see the style he clears a public-house in, in no time !"

" But wouldn't his speaking to them answer the purpose as well ?"

" Oh, no! he doesn't like to throw away his discoorse on thim; and why should he ? he keeps that for the blessed althar on Sunday, which is a fitter place for it; besides, he does not like to be sevare on us."

" Severe ?" said the traveler, in surprise, " why, haven't you said that he thrashes you round on all occasions ?"

" Yis, sir; but what o' that ? sure that's nothin' to his tongue; his words is like swoords or rhazors, I may say; we're used to a lick of a stick every day, but not to sich language as his reverence sometimes murthers us with when we displaze him. Oh! it's terrible, so it is, to have the weight of his tongue on you! Throth! I'd rather let him bate me from this till to-morrow, than have one angry word with him."

" I see, then, he must have a heavy stick," said the traveler.

" To be sure he must, sir, at all times; and that was the raison I was so particular in the shop; and afther spendin' over an hour, would you b'lieve it ? divil a stick I could get in the place fit for a child, much less a man."

" But about the gridiron ?"

" Sure I'm tellin' you about it," said Rory; " only I'm
not come to it yet. You see," continued he, " I was so
disgusted with them shopkeepers in Dublin that my heart
was fairly broke with their ignorance, and I seen they
knew nothin' at all about what I wanted, and so I came
away without anything for his reverence, though it was
on my mind all this day on the road; and comin' through
the last town, in the middle o' the rain, I thought of a
gridiron."

" A very natural thing to think of in a shower of rain,"
said the traveler.

" No, 'twasn't the rain made me think of it. I think it
was God must have put a gridiron in my heart, seein' that
it was a present for the priest I intended; and when I
thought of it, it came into my head, afther, that it would
be a fine thing to sit on, for to keep one out of the rain,
that was ruinatin' my corderoys on the top o' the coach;
so I kept my eye out as we dhrove along up the sthreet,
and sure enough what should I see at a shop half-way
down the town, but a gridiron hanging up at the door!
and so I went back to get it."

" But isn't a gridiron an odd present? hasn't his reverence one already?"

" He had, sir, before it was bruk; but that's what I re-
membered, for I happened to be up at his place one day,
sittin' in the kitchen, when Molly was brilin' some mate
on it for his reverence; and while she jist turned about to
get a pinch o' salt to shake over it, the dog that was in
the place made a dart at the gridiron on the fire, and
threw it down, and up he whips the mate, before one of us
could stop him. With that Molly whips up the gridiron,
and says she, ' Bad luck to you, you disrespectful baste!
would nothin' sarve you but the priest's dinner?' and she
made a crack o' the gridiron at him. ' As you have the
mate, you shall have the gridiron too,' says she; and with

that she gave him such a rap on the head with it, that the bars flew out of it, and his head went through it, and away he pulled it out of her hands, and ran off with the gridiron hangin' round his neck like a necklace; and he went mad a'most with it; for though a kettle to a dog's tail is nathrel, a gridiron round his neck is very surprisin' to him; and away he tatthered over the country, till there wasn't a taste o' the gridiron left together."

MISS MALONY ON THE CHINESE QUESTION.

A Laughable Recitation.

MARY M. DODGE.

Och' don't be talkin'. Is it howld on, ye say? An' didn't I howld on till the heart of me was clane broke entirely, and me wastin' that thin you could clutch me wid yer two hands. To think o' me toilin' like a nager for the six year I've been in Ameriky—bad luck to the day I iver left the owld counthry, to be bate by the likes o' them! (faix an' I'll sit down when I'm ready, so I will, Ann Ryan, an' ye'd better be listnin' than drawin' your remarks) an' it's mysel, with five good characters from respectable places, would be herdin' wid the haythens? The saints forgive me, but I'd be buried alive soon'n put up wid it a day longer. Sure an' I was a granehorn not to be lavin' at onct when the missus kim into me kitchen wid her perlaver about the new waiter-man which was brought out from Californy. "He'll be here the night," says she, "and, Kitty, it's meself looks to you to be kind and patient wid him, for he's a furriner," says she, a kind o' lookin' off. "Sure an' it's little I'll hinder nor interfare wid him nor any other, mum," says I, a kind o' stiff, for I minded me how these French waiters, wid their paper collars and brass rings on their fingers, isn't company for no gurril

brought up dacint and honest. Och! sorra a bit I knew
what was comin' till the missus walked into me kitchen
smilin', and says, kind o' shcared: "Here's Fing Wing,
Kitty, an' you'll have too much sinse to mind his bein' a
little strange." Wid that she shoots the doore; and I,
misthrusting if I was tidied up sufficient for me fine buy
wid his paper collar, looks up and—Holy fathers! may I
niver brathe another breath, but there stud a rale haythen
Chineser a-grinnin' like he'd just come off a tay-box. If
you'll belave me, the crayture was that yeller it 'ud sicken
you to see him; and sorra stich was on him but a black ·
night-gown over his trowsers and the front of his head
shaved claner nor a copper biler, and a black tail a-hang-
in' down from behind, wid his two feet stook into tho
heathenesest shoes you ever set eyes on. Och! but I was
up-stairs afore you could turn about, a-givin' the missus
warnin'; an' only stopt wid her by her raisin' me wages
two dollars, and playdin' wid me how it was a Christian's
duty to bear wid haythins and taitch 'em all in our power
—the saints save us! Well, the ways and trials I had wid
that Chineser, Ann Ryan, I couldn't be tellin'. Not a
blissed thing cud I do but he'd be lookin' on wid his eyes
cocked up'ard like two poomp-handles, an' he widdout a
speck or a smitch o' whiskers on him, and his finger-nails
full a yard long. But it's dying you'd be to see the missus
a-larnin' him, and he grinnin' an' waggin' his pig-tail
(which was pieced out long wid some black stoof, the haythen chate!) and gettin' into her ways wonderful quick, I
don't deny, imitatin' that sharp, you'd be shurprised, and
ketchin' and copyin' things the best of us will do a-hurried
wid work, yet don't want comin' to the knowledge of tho
family—bad luck to him!

Is it ate wid him? Arrah, an' would I be sittin' wid a
haythen and he a-atin' wid drumsticks—yes, an' atin' dogs
an' cats unknownst to me, I warrant you, which is the
custom of them Chineserss, till the thought made me that

sick I could die. An' didn't the crayter proffer to help me
a wake ago come Toosday, an' me a-foldin' down me clane
clothes for the ironin', an' fill his haythen mouth wid water,
an' afore I could hinder squrrit it through his teeth stret
over the best linen table-cloth, and foid it up tight as in-
nercent now as a baby, the dirty baste! But the worrest
of all was the copyin' he'd be doin' till ye'd be dishtracted.
It's yerself knows the tinder feet that's on me since ever
I've bin in this country. Well, owin' to that, I fell into
the way o' slippin' me shoes off when I'd be settin'
down to pale the praties or the likes o' that, and, do ye
mind, that haythin would do the same thing after me
whiniver the missus set him parin' apples or tomaterses.
The saints in heaven couldn't have made him belave he
cud kape the shoes on him when he'd be payling anything.

Did I lave fur that? Faix an' didn't he get me into
trouble wid my missus, the haythin! You're aware yerself how the boondles comin' in from the grocery often contains more 'n 'll go into anything dacently. So, for that
matter, I'd now and then take out a sup o' sugar, or flour,
or tay, an' wrap it in paper and put it in me bit of a box
tucked under the ironin' blankit the how it cuddent be
bodderin' any one. Well, what should it be, but this
blessed Sathurday morn the missus was a spakin' pleasant
and respec'ful wid me in me kitchen when the grocer boy
comes in an' stands fornenst her wid his boondles an' she
motions like to Fing Wing (which I never would call him
by that name nor any other but just haythin), she motions
to him, she does, for to take the boondles an' empty out
the sugar an' what not where they belongs. If you'll belave me, Ann Ryan, what did that blatherin' Chineser do
but take out a sup o' sugar, an' a handful o' tay, an' a bit
o' chaze, right afore the missus, wrap them into bits o'
paper, an' I spacheless wid shuprise, an' he the next
minute up wid the ironin' blanket and pullin' out me box

wid a show o' bein' sly to put them in. Och, the Lord forgive me, but I clutched it, and the missus sayin', "O
Kitty!" in a way that 'ud curdle your blood. "He's a
haythin nager," says I. "I've found you out," says she.
"I'll arrist him," says I. "It's you ought to be arristed,"
says she. "You won't," says I. "I will," says she; and
so it went till she gave me such sass as I cuddent take
from no lady, an' I give her warnin' an' left that instant,
an' she a-pointin' to the doore.

PADDY'S DREAM.

I have often laughed at the way an Irish help we had at
Barnstaple once fished me for a glass of whisky. One
morning he says to me—"Oh, yer honor," says he, "I had
a great drame last night intirely—I dramed I was in Rome,
tho' how I got there is more than I can tell: but there I
was, sure enough; and as in duty bound, what does I do
but go and see the Pope. Well, it was a long journey,
and it was late when I got there—too late for the likes of
me; and when I got to the palace I saw priests, and
bishops, and cardinals, and all the great dignitaries of the
Church a-coming out; and sais one of them to me, 'How
are ye, Pat Moloney?' sais he; 'and that spalpeen your
father, bad luck to him, how is he?' It startled me to
hear me own name so suddint, that it came mighty nigh
waking me up, it did. Sais I, 'Your riverence, how in the
world did ye know that Pat Moloney was me name, let
alone that of me father?' 'Why, ye blackguard,' sais he,
'I knew ye since ye was knee-high to a goose, and I knew
yer mother afore ye was born.' 'It's good right yer honor
has then to know me,' sais I. 'Bad manners to ye,' sais
he, 'what is it ye are after doing here at this time o'
night?' 'To see his Holiness the Pope,' sais I. 'That's
right,' sais he; 'pass on, but leave yer impudence with

yer hat and shoes at the door.' Well, I was shown into a
mighty fine room where his Holiness was, and down I
went on me knees. ' Rise up, Pat Moloney,' sais his Holiness; ' ye're a broth of a boy to come all the way from
Ireland to do yer duty to me; and it's dutiful children ye
are, every mother's son of ye. What will ye have to drink,
Pat?' (The greater a man is, the more of a rael gintleman he is, yer honor, and the more condescending.)
' What will ye have to drink, Pat?' sais he. ' A glass of
whisky, yer Holiness,' sais I, ' if it's all the same to ye.'
' Shall it be hot or cold?' sais he. ' Hot,' sais I, ' if it's
all the same, and gives ye no trouble.' ' Hot it shall be,'
sais he; ' but as I have dismissed all me servants for the
night, I'll just step down below for the tay-kettle;'—and
wid that he left the room, and was gone for a long time;
and jist as he came to the door again he knocked so loud
the noise woke me up, and, be jabers! I missed me whisky
entirely! Bedad, if I had only had the sense to say ' Nate,
yer Holiness,' I'd a had me whisky sure enough, and
never known it warn't all true, instead of a drame." I
knew what he wanted, so I poured him out a glass.
" Won't it do as well now, Pat?" said I. " Indeed it will,
yer honor," says he, " and me drame will come true, after
all. I thought it would, for it was mighty nateral at the
time, all but the whisky."

THE IRISH DRUMMER.

An Irish Recitation.

A soldier, so at least the story goes,
  It was in Ireland, I believe,
    Upon his back was sentenc'd to receive
Five hundred cat-o'-nine-tail blows;
Most sagely military law providing,
The *back* alone shall suffer for *backsliding.*
Whether his crime was great or small,

Or whether there was any crime at all,
   Are facts which this deponent never knew;
But though uncertain whether justly tried,
The man he knows was to the halbert tied,
   And hopes his readers will believe so too.
Suppose him, then, fast to the halberts bound,
His poor companions standing silent round,
   Anticipating ev'ry dreadful smack;
While Patrick Donovan, from Wicklow county,
Is just preparing to bestow his bounty,
   Or *beat quick time* upon his comrade's back.
Of stoics much we read in tales of yore,
   Of Zeno, Possidonius, Epictetus,
Who, unconcerned, the greatest torments bore,
   Or else these ancient stories strangely cheat us.
My hero was no stoic, it is plain:
   He could not suffer torments and be dumb,
But roared, before he felt the smallest pain,
   As though a rusty nail had pierc'd his thumb.
Not louder is the terror-spreading note
Which issues from the hungry lion's throat
When o'er Numidian plains in search of prey
He takes his cruel and destroying way.
The first two strokes, which made my hero bleat,
Fell right across the confines of his seat,
   On which he piteously began to cry,
"Strike high! strike high! for mercy's sake strike high!"
Pat, of a mild, obliging disposition,
Could not refuse to grant his friend's petition;
An Irishman has got a tender heart,
And never likes to act a cruel part;
Pat gave a good example to beholders,
And the next stroke fell on his comrade's shoulders!
Our suffering hero now began to roar
As loud, if not much louder, than before;
At which Pat lost all patience, and exclaim'd,
While his Hibernian face with anger flam'd,
"Perdition catch you!—can't your tongue be still?
There is no *plasing* you, strike where one will!"

PADDY THE PIPER.

SAMUEL LOVER.

Abridged for Public Reading.

I'll tell you, sir, a mighty quare story. 'Twas afther nightfall, and we wor sittin' round the fire, and the pratees was boilin', and the noggins of butthermilk was standin' ready for our suppers, whin a knock kem to the door. "Whist," says my father, "here's the sogers come upon us now," says he. "Bad luck to thim, the villains; I'm afeard they seen a glimmer of the fire through the crack in the door," says he.

"No," says my mother, "for I'm afther hangin' an ould sack and my new petticoat agin it, a while ago."

"Well, whist, anyhow," says my father, "for there's a knock agin;" and we all held our tongues till another thump kem to the door.

"Oh, it's folly to purtind any more," says my father; "they're too cute to be put off that-a-way," says he. "Go, Shamus," says he to me, "and see who's in it."

"How can I see who's in it in the dark?" says I.

"Well," says he, "light the candle, thin, and see who's in it. But don't open the door for your life, barrin' they break it in," says he, "exceptin' to the sojers; and spake them fair, if it's thim."

So with that I wint to the door, and there was another knock.

"Who's there?" says I.

"It's me," says he.

"Who are you?" says I.

"A friend," says he.

"*Baithershin!*" says I; "who are you, at all?"

"Arrah! don't you know me?" says he.

"Divil a taste," says I.

"Sure I'm Paddy the Piper," says he.

"Oh, thundher and turf!" says I; "is it you, Paddy, that's in it?"

" Sorra one else," says he.

" And what brought you at this hour?" says I.

" By gar," says he, " I didn't like goin' the roun' by the road," says he, "and so I kem the short cut, and that's what delayed me," says he.

   *   *   *   *   *   *   *

" Faix, then," says I, " you had betther lose no time in hidin' yourself," says I, "for throth I tell you, it's a short thrial and a long rope the Husshians would be afther givin' you—for they've no justice, and less marcy, the villains!"

" Faith, thin, more's the raison you should let me in, Shamus," says poor Paddy.

" It's a folly to talk," says I ; " I darn't open the door."

" Oh then, millia murther!" says Paddy, " what'll become of me at all, at all?" says he.

" Go aff into the shed," says I, " behind the house, where the cow is ;" but instead of going to the cow-house, he set off to go to the fair, and he went meandherin' along through the fields, but he didn't go far, until climbin' up through a hedge, when he was comin' out at t'other side, he kem plump agin somethin' that made the fire flash out iv his eyes. So with that he looks up—and what do you think it was, Lord be marciful unto uz ! but a corpse hangin' out of a branch of a three? " Oh, the top of the mornin' to you, sir," says Paddy ; " and is that the way with you, my poor fellow? Throth you took a start out o' me," says poor Paddy ; and 'twas thrue for him, for it would make the heart of a stouter man nor Paddy jump to see the like, and to think of a Christian crathur being hanged up, all as one as a dog.

   *   *   *   *   *   *   *

Says Paddy, eyein' the corpse, " By my sowl thin, but you have a beautiful pair of boots an you," says he, " and it's what I'm thinkin' you won't have any great use for thim no more ; and shure it's a shame to see the likes o' me," says he, " the best piper in the sivin counties, to be trampin' wid a pair of ould brogues not worth three *traneens,* and a corpse wid such an illigant pair o' boots, that wants some one to wear thim." So with that Paddy laid hould of him by the boots, and began a pullin' at thim, but they wor mighty stiff; and whether it was by rayson of their bein' so tight, or the branch of the tree a-jiggin' up and down, all as one as a weighdee buckettee, and not lettin' Paddy cotch any right hoult o' thim, he could get no *advantage* o' thim at all ; and at last he gave it up, and was goin' away, whin, lookin' behind him agin, the sight of the illigant fine boots was too much for him, and he turned back . . . . . . outs with his knife, and what does he do, but he cuts off the legs av the corpse ; and says he, "I can take aff the boots at my convanyience." And throth it was, as I said before, a dirty turn.

Well, sir, he tucked up the legs undher his arm, and walked back agin to the cow-house, and hidin' the corpse's legs in the sthraw, Paddy wint to sleep. But what do you think ? the divil a long Paddy was there antil the sojers kem in airnest, and, by the powers, they carried off Paddy ; and faith it was only sarvin' him right for what he had done to the poor corpse.

Well, whin the morning kem, my father says to me, " Go, Shamus," says he, " to the shed, and bid poor Paddy come in, and take share o' the pratees; for I go bail he's ready for his breakquest by this, anyhow."

Well, out I wint to the cow-house, and called out, " Paddy !" and afther callin' three or four times, and gettin' no answer, I wint in, and called agin, and divil an answer I got still. " Blood-an-agers !" says I, " Paddy, where are you, at all, at all ?" and so, castin' my eyes about the shed, I seen two feet sticking out from undher the hape o' straw. " Musha ! thin," says I, " bad luck to you, Paddy, but you're fond of a warm corner ; and maybe you haven't made yourself as snug as a flay in a blanket ? But I'll disturb your dhrames, I'm thinkin'," says I, and

with that, I laid hould of his heels (as I thought), and
givin' a good pull to waken him, as I intindid, away I
wint, head over heels, and my brains was a'most knocked
out agin the wall.   Well, whin I recovered myself, there I
was, on the broad o' my back, and two things stickin' out
o' my hands, like a pair of Husshian's horse-pistils; and I
thought the sight 'd lave my eyes whin I seen they wor
two mortial legs.   My jew'l, I threw thim down like a hot
pratee, and jumpin' up, I roared out millia murther.
" Oh, you murtherin' villain," says I, shaking my fist at
the cow—" Oh, you unnath'ral baste," says I; " you've
ate poor Paddy, you thievin' cannable; you're worse than
a neyger," says I.   " And bad luck to you, how dainty you
are, that nothin' 'd serve you for your suppor but the best
piper in Ireland !"

*   *   *   *   *   *   *

With that I ran out, for throth I didn't like to be near
her; and goin' into the house, I tould them all about it.
" Arrah ! be aisy," says my father.
" Bad luck to the lie I tell you," says I.
" Is it ate Paddy ?" says they.
" Divil a doubt of it," says I.
" Are you sure, Shamus ?" says my mother.
" I wish I was as sure of a new pair of brogues," says I.
" Bad luck to the bit she has left iv him but his two legs."
" And do you tell me that she ate the pipes, too ?" says
my father.
" By gar, I b'lieve so," says I.
" Oh, the divil fly away wid her," says he; " what a
cruel taste she has for music !"
" Arrah !" says my mother, " don't be cursing the cow
that gives milk to the childer."
" Yis, I will," says my father; " why shouldn't I curse
sitch an unnath'ral baste ?"
" You oughtn't to curse any livin' that's undher your
roof," says my mother.

"By my sowl, thin," says my father, "she shan't be undher my roof any more ; for I'll send her to the fair this minit," says he, "and sell her for whatever she'll bring. Go aff," says he, "Shamus, the minit you've ate your breakquest, and dhrive her to the fair."

"Troth, I don't like to dhrive her," says I.

"Arrah, don't be makin' a gommagh of yourself," says he.

"Faith, I don't," says I.

"Well, like or no like," says he, "you must dhrive her."

*   *   *   *   *   *   *

Well, away we wint along the road, and mighty throng'd it wuz wid the boys and the girls, and, in short, all sorts, rich and poor, high and low, crowdin' to the fair.

"God save you," says one to me.

"God save you, kindly," says I.

"That's a fine beast you're dhrivin'," says he.

"Troth she is," says I; though God knows it wint agin my heart to say a good word for the likes of her. . . . I dhriv her into the thick av the fair, whin all of a suddint, as I kem to the door av a tint, up sthruck the pipes to the tune av 'Tatthorin' Jack Walsh,' and, my jew'l, in a minit, the cow cock'd her ears, and was makin' a dart at the tint.

"Oh, murther !" says I to the boys standin' by ; "hould her," says I, "hould her—she ate one piper already, the vagabone, and bad luck to her, she wants another now."

"Is it a cow for to ate a piper ?" says one o' thim.

"Divil a word o' lie in it, for I seen it's corpse myself, and nothin' left but the two legs," says I; "and it's a folly to be sthrivin' to hide it, for I *see* she'll never lave it off— as Poor Paddy Grogan knows to his cost, Lord be marciful to him."

"Who's that takin' my name in vain ?" says a voice in the crowd; and with that, shovin' the throng a one side, who the divil should I see but Paddy Grogan, to all appearance.

"Oh, hould him too," says I; "keep him aff me, for it's not himself at all, but his ghost," says I; "for he was kilt last night, to my sartin knowledge, every inch av him, all to his legs."

Well, sir, with that, Paddy—for it was Paddy himself, as it kem out afther—fell a-laughin' so that you'd think his sides 'ud split. And whin he kem to himself, he ups and he tould us how it was, as I tould you already. And av coorse the poor slandered cow was dhruv home agin, and many a quiet day she had wid uz afther that; and whin she died, throth, my father had sich a regard for the poor thing that he had her skinned, and an illigant pair of breeches made out iv her hide, and it's in the fam'ly to this day. And isn't it mighty remarkable, what I'm going to tell you now, but it's as thrue as I'm here, that from that out, any one that has thim breeches an, the minit a pair o' pipes sthrikes up, they can't rest, but goes jiggin' and jiggin' in their sate, and never stops as long as the pipes is playin'—and there, there is the very breeches that's an me now, and a fine pair they are this minit.

PAT AND THE GRIDIRON.

A Popular Irish Recitation.

SAMUEL LOVER.

It was the time I was lost in crassin' the broad Atlantic, a-comin' home, whin the winds began to blow, and the sae to rowl, that you'd think the *Colleen Dhas* (that was her name) would not have a mast left but what would rowl out of her.

Well, sure enough, the masts went by the board, at last, and the pumps were choak'd (divil choak them for that same), and av coorse the water gained an us; and troth, to be filled with water is neither good for man or baste; and she was sinkin' fast, settlin' down, as the sailors call; and faith I never was good at settlin' down in my life, and I liked it then less nor ever; accordingly we prepared for the worst and put out the boat, and got a sack o' bishkits and a cask o' pork, and a kag o' wather, and a thrifle o' rum aboord, and any other little matthers we could think iv in the mortial hurry we wor in—and faith there was no time to be lost, for, my darlint, the *Colleen Dhas* went down like a lump o' lead, afore we wor many sthrokes o' the oar away from her.

Well, we dhrifted away all that night, and next mornin' we put up a blanket an the end av a pole as well as we could, and then we sailed iligant; for we darn't show a stitch o' canvas the night before, bekase it was blowin' like bloody murther, savin' your presence, and sure it's the wondher of the world we worn't swally'd alive by the ragin' sae.

Well, away we wint, for more nor a week, and nothin' before our two good-lookin' eyes but the canophy iv heaven, and the wide ocean—the broad Atlantic; not a thing was to be seen but the sae and the sky; and though the sae and the sky is mighty purty things in themselves, throth they're no great things when you've nothin' else to look at for a week together—and the barest rock in the world, so it was land, would be more welkim. And then, soon enough, throth, our provisions began to run low, the bishkits, and the wather, and the rum—throth *that* was gone first of all —God help uz—and oh! it was thin that starvation began to stare us in the face—"Oh, murther, murther, captain darlint," says I, "I wish we could land anywhere," says I.

"More power to your elbow, Paddy, my boy," says he, "for sitch a good wish, and throth it's myself wishes the same."

"Och," says I, "that it may plaze you, sweet Queen iv Heaven, supposing it was only a *dissolute* island," says I, "inhabited wid Turks, sure they wouldn't be such bad Christians as to refuse us a bit and a sup."

"Whisht, whisht, Paddy," says the captain, "don't be

talking bad of any one," says he; "you don't know how
soon you may want a good word put in for yourself, if you
should be called to quarthers in th' other world all of a
suddint," says he.

"Thrue for you, captain darlint," says I—I called him
darlint, and made free with him, you see, bekase disthress
makes us all equal—"thrue for you, captain jewel—I owe
no man any spite"—and throth that was only thruth.
Well, the last bishkit was sarved out, and by gor the
wather itself was all gone at last, and we passed the night
mighty cowld—well, at the brake o' day the sun riz most
beautifully out to the waves, that was as bright as silver
and as clear as crystal. But it was only the more cruel
upon us, for we wor beginnin' to feel *terrible* hungry; when
all at wanst I thought I spied the land—by gor I thought
I felt my heart up in my throat in a minit, and "Thunder
an' turf, captain," says I, "look to leeward," says I.

"What for?" says he.

"I think I see the land," says I. So he ups with his
bring-'em-near (that's what the sailors call a spy-glass,
sir) and looks out, and, sure enough, it was.

"Hurra!" says he, "we're all right now; pull away, my
boys," says he.

"Take care you're not mistaken," says I; "maybe it's
only a fog-bank, captain darlint," says I.

"Oh, no," says he, "it's the land in airnest."

"Oh, then, whereabouts in the wide world are we, captain?" says I; "maybe it id be *Roosia,* or *Proosia,* or the
Garman Oceant," says I.

"Tut, you fool," says he—for he had that consaited way
wid him—thinkin' himself cleverer nor any one else—"tut,
you fool," says he, "that's *France,*" says he.

"Tare an' ouns," says I, "do you tell me so? and how
do you know it's France it is, captain dear?" says I.

"Bekase this is the Bay o' Bishky we're in now," says
he.

" Throth, I was thinkin' so myself," says I, " by the rowl it has; for I often heerd av it in regard of that same; and throth the likes av it I never seen before nor since."

Well, with that, my heart began to grow light; and when I seen my life was safe, I began to grow twice hungrier nor ever—so, says I, " Captain, jewel, I wish we had a gridiron."

" Why, then," says he, " thunder an' turf," says he, " what puts a gridiron into your head ?"

" Bekase I'm starvin' with the hunger," says I.

" And sure, bad luck to you," says he, " you couldn't eat a gridiron," says he, " barrin' you were a *pelican o' the wildherness*," says he.

" Ate a gridiron," says I ; " och, in throth I'm not such a *gommoch* all out as that, anyhow. But sure, if we had a gridiron, we could dress a beef-steak," says I.

" Arrah ! but where's the beef-steak," says he.

" Sure, couldn't we cut a slice aff the pork ?" says I.

" Be gor, I never thought o' that," says the captain. " You're a clever fellow, Paddy," says he, laughin'.

" Oh, ther's many a thrue word said in joke," says I.

" Thrue for you, Paddy," says he.

" Well, thin," says I, " if you put me ashore there beyant," [for we were nearin' the land all the time,] " and sure I can ax them for to lind me the loan of a gridiron," says I.

" Oh, by gor, the butther's comin' out o' the stirabout in airnest now," says he, " you gommoch," says he, " sure I told you before that's France—and sure the're all furriners there," says the captain.

" Well," says I, " and how do you know but I'm as good a furriner myself as any o' thim ?"

" What do you mane ?" says he.

" I mane," says I, " what I towld you, that I'm as good a furriner myself as any o' thim."

" Make me sinsible," says he.

" By dad, maybe that's more nor me, or greater nor me, could do," says I—and we all began to laugh at him, for I thought I would pay him off for his bit o' consait about the Garmant Ocean.

" Lave aff your humbuggin'," says he, " I bid you, and tell me what it is you mane, at all at all."

" *Parley voo frongsay ?*" says I.

" Oh, your humble sarvant," says he ; " why, by gor, you're a scholar, Paddy."

" Throth, you may say that," says I.

" Why, you're a clever fellow, Paddy," says the captain, jeerin' like.

" You're not the first that said that," says I, "whether you joke or no."

" Oh, but I'm in airnest," says the captain—" and do you tell me, Paddy," says he, " that you speak Frinch ?"

" *Parly voo frongsay ?*" says I.

" By gor, that bangs Banagher, and all the world knows Banagher bangs the divil—I never met the likes o' you, Paddy," says he—" pull away, boys, and put Paddy ashore, and maybe we won't get a bellyful before long."

So, with that, it was no sooner said nor done—they pulled away, and got close in to shore in less than no time, and run the boat up in a little creek, and a beautiful creek it was, with a lovely white sthrand—an illegant place for ladies to bathe in the summer—and out I got ; and it's stiff enough in the limbs I was, afther bein' cramped up in the boat, and perished with the cowld and hunger, but I conthrived to scramble on, one way or t'other, tow'rds a little bit iv a wood that was close to the shore, and the smoke curlin' out iv it, quite timptin' like.

" By the powdhers o' war, I'm all right," says I ; " there's a house there,"—and sure enough there was, and a parcel of men, women and childher, ating their dinner round a table, quite convanient. And so I wint up to the door, and I thought I'd be very civil to them, as I heered the

PAT AND THE GRIDIRON.

French was always mighty p'lite intirely—and I thought I'd show them I knew what good manners was.

So, I took aff my hat, and, makin' a low bow, says I, "God save all here," says I.

Well to be sure, they all stapt eatin' at wanst, and began to stare at me; and faith they almost looked me out of countenance—and I thought to myself, it was not good manners at all—more betoken from furriners, which they call so mighty p'lite; but I never minded that, in regard o' wantin' the gridiron; and so, says I, "I beg your pardon," says I, "for the liberty I take, but it's only bein' in disthress in regard of eatin'," says I, "that I made bowld to throuble yez, and if you could lind me the loan of a gridiron," says I, "I'd be entirely obleeged to ye."

By gor, they all stared at me twice worse nor before—and with that, says I (knowin' what was in their minds), "Indeed it's thrue for you," says I, "I'm tatthered to pieces, and I look quare enough; but it's by raison of the storm," says I, "which dhruv us ashore here below, and we're all starvin'," says I.

So then they began to look at each other again, and myself, seein' at once dirty thoughts was in their heads, and that they tuk me for a poor beggar, comin' to crave charity; with that, says I, "O, not at all," says I, "by no manes—we have plenty of mate ourselves there below, and we'll dhress it," says I, "if you would be pleased to lind us the loan of a gridiron," says I, makin' a low bow.

Well, sir, with that, throth they stared at me twice worse nor ever, and faith I began to think that maybe the captain was wrong, and that it was not France at all, at all; and so says I : "I beg pardon, sir," says I, to a fine ould man, with a head of hair as white as silver, "maybe I'm under a mistake," says I, "but I thought I was in France, sir; aren't you furriners?" says I, "*parley voo frongsay?*"

"*We, munseer,*" says he.

" Then, would you lind me the loan of a gridiron," says
I, " if you plase ?"

Oh, it was thin that they stared at me, as if I had seven
heads; and, faith, myself began to feel flushed like and
onaisy, and so says I, makin' a bow and scrape agin, " I
know it's a liberty I take, sir, but it's only in the regard of
bein' cast away; and if you plase, sir," says I, "*parley voo
frongsay ?*"

"*We, munseer,*" says he, mighty sharp.

" Then, would you lind me the loan of a gridiron," says
I, " and you'll obleege me."

Well, sir, the ould chap began to munseer me; but the
devil a bit of a gridiron he'd gi' me, and so I began to
think they wor all neygars, for all their fine manners; and
throth, my blood began to rise, and says I, " By my sowl,
if it was you was in distriss," says I, " and if it was to ould
Ireland you kem, it's not only the gridiron they'd give
you, if you axed it, but something to put on it, too, and
the drop o' drink into the bargain, and *caed mile failte.*"

Well, the word *caed mile failte* seemed to sthreck his
heart, and the old chap cocked his ear, and so I thought
I'd give him another offer, and make him sensible at last;
and so says I, wanst more, quite slow, that he might understand, "*Parley voo frongsay, munseer ?*"

"*We, munseer,*" says he.

" Then lind me the loan of a gridiron," says I, " and bad
scram to you."

Well, bad win to the bit of it he'd gi' me, and the ould
chap begins bowin' and scrapin', and said something or
other about long-tongs.*

" Phoo!—the divil swape yourself and your tongs," says
I; " I don't want a tongs at all, at all; but can't you listen to raison ?" says I. "*Parley voo frongsay ?*"　·

"*We, munseer.*"

---

* Some mystification of Paddy's touching the French *n'entends.*

" Then lind me the loan of a gridiron," says **I,** " and howld your prate."

Well, what would you think, but he shook his ould noddle, as much as to say he wouldn't; and so says I, " Bad cess to the likes o' that I ever seen—throth if you wor in my counthry it's not that-a-way they'd use you. The curse o' the crows an you, you owld sinner," says I, " the divil a longer I'll darken your door."

So he seen I was vexed, and I thought, as I was turnin' away, I seen him begin to relint, and that his conscience throubled him; and says I, turnin' back, " Well, I'll give one chance more, you ould thief: Are you a Chrishthan at all—are you a furriner," says I, " that all the world calls so p'lite ? Bad luck to you, do you understand your own language ? *Parley voo frongsay ?"* says I.

" We, munseer," says he.

" Then, thunder an' turf," says I, " will you lind me the loan of a gridiron ?"

Well, sir, the devil resave the bit of it he'd gi' me, and so with that, " The curse o' the hungry an you, you ould negarly villain !" says I; " the back o' my hand, and the sowl o' my foot to you, that you may want a gridiron yourself, yit," says I; and with that I left them there, sir, and kem away—and, in troth, it's often since that I *thought that it was remarkable.*

HOW DENNIS TOOK THE PLEDGE.

A Limerick Irishman named Dennis, addicted to strong drink, was often urged by his friends to sign the pledge, but with no avail, until one day they read to him from a newspaper an account of a man who had become so thoroughly saturated with alcohol, that, on attempting to blow out a candle, his breath ignited, and he was instantly blown to atoms. Dennis's face showed mingled horror and contrition, and his friends thought that the long-desired moment of repentance was at hand.

"Bring me the book, boys, bring me the book! Troth, his breath took foir, did it? Sure, I'll niver die that death, onyhow," said Dennis, with the most solemn countenance imaginable. "Hear me now, b'ys, hear me now. I, Dennis Finnegan, knowin' my great weakness, deeply sinsible of my past sins, an' the great danger I've been in, hereby take me solemn oath, that, so long as I live, under no provocation whativer, will I—*blow out a candil again!*"

PADDY O'RAFTHER.

SAMUEL LOVER.

Paddy, in want of a dinner one day,
Credit all gone, and no money to pay,
Stole from the priest a fat pullet, they say,
    And went to confession just afther;
"Your riv'rince," says Paddy, "I stole this fat hen."
"What, what!" says the priest, "at your owld thricks again?
Faith, you'd rather be stealin' than sayin' amen,
                Paddy O'Rafther!"

"Sure you wouldn't be angry," says Pat, "if you knew
That the best of intintions I had in my view,
For I stole it to make it a present to you,
    And you can absolve me afther."
"Do you think," says the priest, "I'd partake of your theft?
Of your seven small senses you must be bereft—
You're the biggest blackguard that I know, right or left,
                Paddy O'Rafther!"

"Then what shall I do with the pullet," says Pat,
"If your riv'rince won't take it?—By this and by that
I don't know no more than a dog nor a cat
    What your riv'rince would have me be afther."
"Why, then," says his rev'rence, "you sin-blinded owl,
Give back, to the man that you stole from, his fowl,
For if you do not, 'twill be worse for your sowl,
                Paddy O'Rafther!"

Says Paddy, " I asked him to take it—'tis thrue
As this minit I'm talkin', your riv'rince, to you;
But he wouldn't resaive it—so what can I do ?"
    Says Paddy, nigh chokin' with laughter.
" By my throth," says the priest, " but the case is absthruse;
If he won't take his hen, why the man is a goose—
'Tis not the first time my advice was no use,
                    Paddy O'Rafther !

" But for the sake of your sowl, I would sthrongly advise
To some one in want you would give your supplies,
Some widow, or orphan, with tears in their eyes,
    And then you may come to me afther."
So Paddy went off to the brisk Widow Hoy,
And the pullet, between them, was eaten with joy.
And, says she, " 'Pon my word you're the cleverest boy,
                    Paddy O'Rafther !"

Then Paddy went back to the priest, the next day,
And told him the fowl he had given away
To a poor lonely widow, in want and dismay,
    The loss of her spouse weeping after.
" Well, now," says the priest, " I'll absolve you, my lad,
For repentantly making the best of the bad,
In feeding the hungry and cheering the sad,
                    Paddy O'Rafther !"

PAT AND HIS MUSKET.

An Irish Recitation.

I've heard a good joke of an Emerald Pat,
Who kept a few brains and a brick in his hat.
He was bound to go hunting; so, taking his gun,
He rammed down a charge—this was load number one
Then put in the priming, and when all was done,
By way of experiment, thought he would try
And see if perchance he might hit the " bull's eye."
He straightened himself till he made a good figure,
Took deliberate aim, and then pulled the trigger.
Click ! went the hammer, but nothing exploded;
" And sure," muttered Paddy, " the gun isn't loaded !"

So down went another charge, just as before,
Unless this contained just a grain or two more.
" I wonder can this be still shootin'?" said Pat;
" I'll put down a load now, I'm certain of that;
I'll try it again, and then we shall see!"
So down went the cartridge of load number three!
Then trying again, with a confident air,
And succeeding no better, gave up in despair.
Just at that moment, he happened to spy
His friend, Michael Milligan, hurrying by.
" Hollo, Mike! come here, and just try on my gun;
I've been tryin' to shoot till I'm tired and done!"
So Mike took the gun, and pricked up the powder,
Remarking to Pat, " It would make it go louder;"
Then placing it firmly against his right arm,
And never suspecting it might do him harm,
He pointed the piece in the proper direction,
And pulled on the trigger without more reflection—
When, off went the gun! like a country election,
Where whisky and gin have exclusive selection
Of those who are chosen to guard the inspection
(There's a great deal of noise—and some little inspection)
And Michael " went off" in another direction!
" Hold on!" shouted Pat, " Hold on to the gun!
I put in three loads, and you've fired off but one!
Get up, and be careful—don't hold it so level,
Or else we are both of us gone to the devil!"
" I'm going," says Michael, " it's time that I wint,
I've got myself kicked, and it's time for the hint."

THE IRISH PHILOSOPHER.

A Favorite Irish Recitation.

LADIES AND GINTLEMEN:—I see so many foine-lookin'
people sittin' before me, that if you'll excuse me I'll be
after takin' a seat meself.

You don't know me, I'm thinkin', or some of yees 'ud be
noddin' to me afore this.

I'm a walkin' pedestrian, a traveling philosopher; Terry O'Mulligan's me name. I'm from Dublin, where many philosophers before me was raised and bred. Oh, philosophy is a foine study. I don't know anything about it, but it's a foine study. Before I *kim* over I attinded an important meetin' of philosophers in Dublin, and the discussin' and talkin' you'd hear there about the world 'ud warm the very heart of Socrates or Aristotle himself. Well, there was a great many *imminent* and learned min there at the meetin', and I was there too, and while we was in the very thickest of a heated argument a man comes up to me, and says he, "Do you know what we're talkin' about?" "I do," says I, "but I don't understand yees." "Could you explain the sun's motion round the earth?" says he. "I could," says I; "but I'd not know could you understand me or not." "Well," says he, "we'll see," says he.

Sure 'n I didn't know anything how to get out of it then, so I piled in, for says I to meself, never let on to any one that you don't know anything, but make them believe that you do know all about it. So says I to him, takin' up me shillalah this way—(*holding a very crooked stick horizontally*)—"We will take that for the straight line of the earth's equator." How's that for gehoggraphy? (*To the audience.*) Oh, that was straight till the other day I bent it in an argument.

"Very good," says he. "Well," says I, "now the sun rises in the east." (*Placing the disengaged hand at the eastern end of the stick.*) Well, he couldn't deny that, "and," says I, "he—he—he rises in the mornin'." No more could he deny that. "Very early," says I, "and when he gets up he

> Darts his rosy beams
> Through the mornin' gleams."

Do you moine the poetry there? (*To the audience, with a smile.*) "And he keeps on risin' an' risin' till he reaches his meridan." "What's that?" says he. "His dinner-toime," says I. "Sure 'n that's my Latin for dinner-toime. And when he gets his dinner

> He sinks to rest
> Behind the glorious hills of the west."

Oh, begorra, there's more poetry. I feel it croppin' out all over me.

"There," says I, well satisfied with meself, "will that do for ye?"

"You haven't got done with him," says he.

"Done with him?" says I, kinder mad like. "What more do you want me to do with him? Didn't I bring him from the east to the west? What more do you want?" "Oh," says he, "you have to have him back agin in the east to rise the next mornin'!"

By Saint Patrick, and wasn't I near betrayin' me ignorance. Sure 'n I thought there was a large family of suns, and they riz one after the other; but I gathered meself quick, and says I to him, "Well," says I, "I'm surprised you ax me that simple question. I thought any man 'ud know," says I, "when the sun sinks to rest in the west that er— When the sun," says I— "You said that before," says he. "Well, I want to impress it strongly upon you," says I. "When the sun sinks to rest behind the glorious hills of the east—no, west—why, he—why, he waits till it grows very dark, and then he *goes back in the night-toime!*"

ST. KEVIN.

SAMUEL LOVER.

A Legend of Glendalough.

At Glendalough lived a young saint,
In odor of sanctity dwelling—
An old-fashion'd odor, which now
We seldom or never are smelling;

A book or a hook were to him
  The utmost extent of his wishes;
Now, a snatch at the " Lives of the Saints;"
  Then, a catch at the lives of the fishes.

There was a young woman, one day,
  Sauntering along by the lake, sir;
She looked hard at St. Kevin, they say,
  But St. Kevin no notice did take, sir.
When she found looking hard wouldn't do,
  She look'd soft—in the old sheep's eye fashion;
But, with all her sheep's eyes, she could not
  In St. Kevin see signs of soft passion.

" You're a great hand at fishing," says Kate;
  " 'Tis yourself that knows how, faith, to hook them;
But, when you have caught them, *agra*,
  Don't you want a young woman to cook them ?"
Says the saint, " I am ' *sayrious inclined*,'
  I intend taking orders for life, dear."
" Only marry," says Kate, " and you'll find
  You'll get orders enough from your wife, dear."

" You shall never be flesh of my flesh,"
  Says the saint, with an anchorite groan, sir;
" I see that myself," answer'd Kate,
  " I can only be ' bone of your bone,' sir.
And even your bones are so scarce,"
  Said Miss Kate, at her answers so glib, sir,
" That I think you would not be the worse
  Of a little additional rib, sir."

The saint, in a rage, seized the lass—
  He gave her one twirl round his head, sir,
And, before Doctor Arnott's invention,
  Prescrib'd her a watery bed, sir.
Oh, cruel St. Kevin !—for shame !
  When a lady her heart came to barter,
You should not have been Knight of the Bath,
  But have bowed to the order of Garter.

THE WIDOW CUMMISKEY.

A Laughable Irish Recitation.

The widow Cummiskey was standing at the door of her little millinery store, Avenue D, the other evening, as Mr. Costello came along. Mr. Costello stopped.

" Good evening to you, ma'am," said he.

" Good evening to you," answered the widow.

" It's fine weather we're havin', ma'am," continued Mr. Costello.

" It is that, thank God," replied Mrs. Cummiskey, "but the winter's comin' at last, and it comes to all, both great and small."

" Ah !" said Mr. Costello, "but for all that it doesn't come to us all alike.   Now, here are you, ma'am, fat, rosy, an' good-lookin', equally swate as a summer greening, a fall pippin, or a winter russet—"

" Arrah, hould yer whist, now," interrupted the fair widow, laughing.   " Much an old bachelor like you knows about apples or women.   But come in, Mr. Costello, and take a cup of tay with me, for I was only standin' be the doore lookin' at the people passin' for company sake, like, and I'm sure the kettle must have sung itself hoarse."

Mr. Costello needed no second invitation, and he followed his hostess into her snug back room.   There was a bright fire burning in the little Franklin stove, the tea-kettle was sending forth a cloud of steam that took a ruddy glow from the fire-light, the shaded light on the table gave a mellow and subdued light to the room, and it was all very suggestive of comfort.

" It's very cosey ye are here, Mrs. Cummiskey," said Mr. Costello, casting a look of approbation around the room.

" Yes," replied the widow, as she laid the supper, "it is that whin I do have company."

" Ah," said Mr. Costello, "it must be lonesome for you with only the cat and yer cup o' tay."

"Sure it is," answered the widow. "But take a sate and set down, Mr. Costello. Help yourself to the fish, an' don't forgit the purtaties. Look at thim; they're splittin' their sides with laughin'."

Mr. Costello helped himself and paused. He looked at the plump widow, with her arms in that graceful position assumed in the pouring out of tea, and remarked, "I'm sinsible of the comforts of a home, Mrs. Cummiskey, although I've none mesilf. Mind, now, the difference between the taste o' the tay made and served that-a-way and the tay they gives you in an 'ating-house."

"Sure," said the widow, "there's nothin' like a home of your own. I wonder ye never got marrit, Mr. Costello."

"I was about to make the same remark in riference to yerself, ma'am," answered Mr. Costello.

"God keep us," exclaimed Mrs. Cummiskey, "aren't I a widder woman this seven year?"

"Ah," rejoined Mr. Costello, "but it's thinkin' I was why ye didn't get marrit again."

"Well, it's sure I am," said the widow, thoughtfully, setting down her tea-cup and raising her hand by way of emphasis, "there never was a better husband to any woman than him that's dead and gone, Heaven save and rest his soul. He was that aisy, a child could do anythin' with him, and he was as humorsome as a monkey. You favor him very much, Mr. Costello; he was about your height, an' dark-complected like you!"

"Ah!" exclaimed Mr. Costello.

"He often used to say to me in his bantherin' way, 'Sure, Nora, what's the worruld to a man whin his wife is a widder?' manin', you know, that all timptations in luxuries of this life can never folly a man beyant the grave. 'Sure, Nora,' says he, 'what's this worruld to a man whin his wife is a widder?' Ah, poor John!"

"It was a sensible sayin', that," remarked Mr. Costello, helping himself to more fish.

" I mind the day John died," continued the widow. " He
knew everything to the last, and about four in the afternoon—it was seventeen minutes past five exactly, be the
clock, that he died—he says to me, 'Nora,' says he,
'you've been a good wife,' says he, ' an' I've been a good
husband,' says he, ' an' so there's no love lost betune us,'
says he, ' an' I could give you a good char-ak-tur to any
place,' says he, ' an' I wish you could do the same for me
where I'm goin',' says he, ' but it's case equal,' says he ;
' every dog has his day, and some has a day and a half,'
says he, 'and,' says he, 'I'll know more in a bit than
Father Corrigan himself,' says he, ' so I'll not bother my
brains about it ;' and he says, says he, ' and if at any time
ye see anny wan ye like better nor me, marry him,' says
he, for the first time spakin' it solemn like. 'Ah, Nora,
what is the wuruld to a man when his wife is a widder ?
And,' says he, ' I lave fifty dollars for masses, and the rest
I lave to yourself,' says he, ' an' I needn't tell ye to be a
good mother to the children,' says he, ' for well we know
there are none.' Ah, poor John. Will ye have another
cup of tay, Mr. Costello ?"

" It must have been very hard on ye," said Mr. Costello.
" Thank ye, ma'am, no more."

" It was hard," said Mrs. Cummiskey; " but time will
tell. I must cast about me for me own livin', an' so I got
until this place, an' here I am to-day."

" Ah !" said Mr. Costello, as they rose from the table
and seated themselves before the fire, " an' here we are
both of us this evenin'."

" Here we are, sure enough," rejoined the widow.

" An' so I mind ye of—of him, do I ?" asked Mr. Costello, after a pause, during which he had gazed contem-
platively into the fire.

" That ye do," answered the widow. " Ye favor him
greatly. Dark-complected an' the same pleasant smile."

" Now, with me sittin' here, and you sittin' there foreninst me, ye might almost think ye were marrit again," said Mr. Costello, insinuatingly.

" Ah, go 'way now for a taze that ye are," exclaimed the widow, mussing her clean apron by rolling up the corners of it.

" I disremember what it was he said about seein' anny man you liked better nor him," said Mr. Costello, moving his chair a little nearer to that of the widow.

" He said, said he," answered the widow, smoothing her apron over her knees with her plump white hands, " ' Nora,' said he, ' if any time ye see anny man ye like better nor me, marry him,' says he."

" Did he say anything about anny wan ye liked as well as him?" asked Mr. Costello.

" I don't mind that he did," answered the widow, re-flectively, folding her hands in her lap.

" I suppose he left that to yerself?" pursued Costello.

" Faith, an' I don't know, thin," answered Mrs. Cum-miskey.

" D'ye think ye like me as well as him?" asked Costello, persuasively, leaning forward to look into the widow's eyes, which were cast down.

" Ah, go 'way for a taze," exclaimed the widow, straight-ening herself, and playfully slapping Costello in the face.

He moved his chair still nearer, and stole his arm around her waist.

" Nivver you think I'm ticklesome, Mr. Costello," says the widow, looking boldly at him.

" Tell me," he insisted, " d'ye like me as well as ye did him?"

" I—I most—I most disremember now how much I liked him," answered the widow, naturally embarrassed by such a question.

" Well, thin," asked Costello, enforcing his question by gentle squeezes of the widow's round waist, " d'ye like me well enough as meself?"

" Hear the man !" exclaimed the widow, derisively ; " do I like him well enough as himself?"

" Ah, now, don't be breakin' me heart," pleaded Costello. "Answer me this question, Mrs. Cummiskey: Is yer heart tender towards me ?"

" It is," whispered the widow; " an' there, now ye have it."

" Glory be to God !" exclaimed the happy lover, and he drew the not unwilling widow to his bosom.

A few minutes after Mrs. Cummiskey looked up, and, as she smoothed her hair, said : " But, Jam—es, ye haven't told me how ye liked yer tay."

" Ah, Nora, me jewel," answered Mr. Costello, " the taste of that first kiss would take away the taste of all the tay that ever was brewed."

"THE IRISHMAN'S PANORAMA."

As recited by J. S. Burdett.

Ladies and gintlemen : In the foreground over thare yer'll observe Vinegar Hill, and should yer be goin' by that way some day, yer moight be fatiguod, an' if yer ar' yer'll foind at the fut o' the hill a nate little cot kept by a man name McCarty, who, be the way, is as foine a lad as you'll mate in a day's march. I see by the hasp on the door that McCarty's out, or I'd take yes in an' introduce yer. A foine, noble, ginerous fellar this McCarty, shure, an' if he had but the wan peratie he'd give yer the half it, an' phot's more, he'd thank yer for takin' it. (Move the crank, James. Music be the bagpipes, Larry.)

Ladies an' gintlemen : We've now arrived at a beautiful shpot, situated about twinty moiles this side o' Limerick. To the left over thare yer'll see a hut be the side of which is sated a lady an' gintleman ; well, as I was goin' that way wan day, the following conversation I heard 'twixt him an' her. Says she to him : " James, it's a shame for yer to be ratin' me so—yer moind the time yer come to me father's castle a-beggin'!" "Yer father's castle, me woife? shure yer could shtand on the outside, stick yer arm down the chimney, pick peraties out o' the pot, and divil a partition betwixt you and the hogs but shtraw!" (Move the crank, James, etc.)

Ladies and gintlemen: We have now arrived at the beautiful and classical Lakes of Killarney. Thare's a curious legend connected wid dese lakes that I must relate to yer. It is that every avenin', at foor o'clock in the afternoon, a beautiful swan is seen to make its appearance, and while movin' along transendently and glidelessly, ducks its limbs, skips under the water, and yer'll not see him again till the next afternoon. (Turn the crank, James, etc.)

Ladies and gintlemen: We have no' arrived at another beautiful shpot, situated about thirteen an' a half miles this side of Coruk. This is a grate place, noted for shportsmen, an' phile shtoppin' over thare at the Hotel de Finney, the following tilt of a conversation occurred betwixt Mr. Muldooney, the waiter, and meself. I says to him, says I, "Mully, ould boy, will you have the kindness to fetch me in the mustard?" an' he was a long time bringin' it, an' I opportuned him for kapin' me, and says he to me, says he, "Mr. McCune (that's me), I notice that you take a great dale of mustard wid your mate." "I do," says I. Says he, "I notice that you take a blame sight of mate wid your mustard." (Move the crank, James, etc.)

Ladies and gintlemen: Before I close my Panáramma, I'll show you one more picture.

While traveling in the States, some years ago, for the benefit of my health, I took the cars for Chin-chin-nat-ti, State of Oh-ho-ho, on me way to Mont-real and Que-bec-que, in Can-a-da, down the river Saint Larry-o-mae, till a place called Buff-lo, after which I struck a party going about eighteen an' a half miles north, till a place celebrated for its great waterfall, an' called Ni-a-ga-ra.

While passin' by the Falls wan evenin' I overheard the followin' remarks pass between a lady an' gintleman. Says he to her, "Mary Ann," says he, "cast your eyes up on that ledge of rocks, and see that vast body of water a-rushin' down over the precipice. Isn't that a great curiosity?" "I know that," says she; "but fou'dent it be a greater curiosity if they'd all turn round and pass back again?"

"James, turn the crank. Larry, give us "Home, Swate Home.")

PADDY BLAKE'S ECHO.

SAMUEL LOVER.

One of the Wonders of Killarney.

In the gap of Dunlo
There's an echo, or so,
And some of them echoes is very surprisin';
You'll think, in a stave
That I mane to desaive,
For a ballad's a thing you expect to find lies in.
But visibly thrue
In that hill forninst you
There's an echo as plain and safe as the bank, too;
But civilly spake
"How d'ye do, Paddy Blake?"
The echo politely says "Very well, thank you!"

One day Teddy Keogh
With Kate Conner did go
To hear from the echo such wondherful talk, sir;
But the echo, they say,
Was conthrairy that day,
Or perhaps Paddy Blake had gone for a walk, sir.
So Ted says to Kate
"'Tis too hard to be bate
By that deaf and dumb baste of an echo, so lazy,
But if we both shout
At each other, no doubt,
We'll make up an echo between us, my daisy!

"Now, Kitty," says Teddy,
"To answer be ready."
" Oh, very well, thank you," cried out Kitty, then, sir.
" Would *you* like to wed,
Kitty darlin' ?" says Ted.
" Oh, very well, thank you," says Kitty, again, sir.
"D'ye like *me* ?" says Teddy,
And Kitty, quite ready,
Cried " Very well, thank you !" with laughter beguiling.
Now won't you confess
Teddy could not do less
Than pay his respects to the lips that were smiling ?

Oh, dear Paddy Blake,
May you never forsake
Those hills that return us such echoes endearing ;
And, girls, all translate
The sweet echoes like Kate,
No faithfulness doubting, no treachery fearing.
And, boys, be you ready,
Like frolicsome Teddy,
Be *earnest* in loving, though given to *joking;*
And thus when inclined,
May all true lovers find
Sweet echoes to answer from hearts they're invoking !

THE WAKE OF TIM O'HARA.

ROBERT BUCHANAN.

To the wake of O'Hara
Came companie ;
All St. Patrick's Alley
Was there to see,
With the friends and kinsmen
Of the family.
On the old deal table Tim lay in white,
And at his pillow the burning light ;
While, pale as himself, with the tear on her cheek,
The mother received us—too full to speak.
But she heap'd the fire, and, with never a word,

Set the black bottle upon the board,
While the company gathered, one and all,
Men and women, big and small—
Not one in the alley but felt a call
          To the wake of Tim O'Hara.

          At the face of O'Hara,
            All white with sleep,
          Not one of the women
            But took a peep,
          And the wives new wedded
            Began to weep.
The mothers clustered around about,
And praised the linen and laying out,
For white as snow was his winding-sheet,
And all looked peaceful, and clean, and sweet.
The old wives, praising the blessèd dead,
Clustered thick round the old press-bed,
Where O'Hara's widow, tattered and torn,
Held to her bosom the babe new-born,
And stared all round her, with eyes forlorn,
          At the wake of Tim O'Hara.

          For the heart of O'Hara
            Was true as gold,
          And the life of O'Hara
            Was bright and bold,
          And his smile was precious
            To young and old.
Gay as a guinea, wet or dry,
With a smiling mouth and a twinkling eye!
Had ever an answer for chaff or fun,
Would fight like a lion with any one!
Not a neighbor of any trade
But knew some joke that the boy had made!
Not a neighbor, dull or bright,
But minded something, frolic or fight,
And whispered it round the fire that night,
          At the wake of Tim O'Hara.

"To God be glory
   In death and life!
He's taken O'Hara
   From trouble and strife,"
Said one-eyed Biddy,
   The apple-wife.
"God bless old Ireland!" said Mistress Hart,
Mother of Mike, of the donkey-cart:
"God bless old Ireland till all be done!
She never made wake for a better son!"
And all joined chorus, and each one said
Something kind of the boy that was dead.
The bottle went round from lip to lip,
And the weeping widow, for fellowship,
Took the glass of old Biddy, and had a sip,
   At the wake of Tim O'Hara.

Then we drank to O'Hara
   With drams to the brim,
While the face of O'Hara
   Looked on so grim,
In the corpse-light shining
   Yellow and dim.
The drink went round again and again;
The talk grew louder at every drain;
Louder the tongues of the women grew;
The tongues of the boys were loosing too!
But the widow her weary eyelids closed,
And, soothed by the drop of drink, she dozed;
The mother brightened and laughed to hear
Of O'Hara's fight with the grenadier,
And the hearts of us all took better cheer,
   At the wake of Tim O'Hara.

Tho' the face of O'Hara
   Looked on so wan,
In the chimney corner
   The row began;
Lame Tony was in it,
   The oyster-man.

For a dirty low thief from the north came near
And whistled "Boyne Water" in his ear,
And Tony, with never a word of grace,
Hit out his fist in the blackguard's face.
Then all the women screamed out for fright;
The men that were drunkest began to fight;
Over the chairs and the tables they threw;
The corpse-light tumbled, the trouble grew;
The new-born joined in the hullabaloo,
     At the wake of Tim O'Hara.

     "Be still! Be silent!
       Ye do a sin!
     Shame be his portion
      Who dares begin!"
    'Twas Father O'Connor
     Just entered in;
And all looked shamed, and the row was done;
Sorry and sheepish looked every one;
But the priest just smiled quite easy and free—
"Would you wake the poor boy from his sleep?" said he.
And he said a prayer, with a shining face,
Till a kind of a brightness filled the place;
The women lit up the dim corpse-light,
The men were quieter at the sight;
And the peace of the Lord fell on all that night,
     At the wake of Tim O'Hara.

FATHER MOLLOY.

SAMUEL LOVER.

The Dying Confession of Paddy McCabe.

Paddy McCabe was dying one day,
   And Father Molloy he came to confess him;
Paddy pray'd hard he would make no delay,
   But forgive him his sins and make haste for to bless him.
"First tell me your sins," says Father Molloy,
"For I'm thinking you've not been a very good boy."

" Oh," says Paddy, " so late in the evenin' I fear
'Twould throuble you such a long story to hear,
For you've ten long miles o'er the mountain to go,
While the road *I've* to travel's much longer, you know:
So give us your blessin' and get in the saddle;
To tell all my sins my poor brain it would addle;
And the docthor gave ordhers to keep me so quiet—
'Twould disturb me to tell all my sins, if I'd thry it—
And your Reverence has towld us unless we tell *all*
'Tis worse than not makin' confession at all:
So I'll say, in a word, I'm no very good boy,
And, therefore, your blessin', sweet Father Molloy."

" Well, I'll read from a book," says Father Molloy,
" The manifold sins that humanity's heir to;
And when you hear those that your conscience annoy,
   You'll just squeeze my hand, as acknowledging thereto."
Then the Father began the dark roll of iniquity,
And Paddy, thereat, felt his conscience grow rickety,
And he gave such a squeeze that the priest gave a roar—
" Oh, murdher !" says Paddy, " don't read any more;
For, if you keep readin', by all that is thrue,
Your Reverence's fist will be soon black and blue;
Besides, to be troubled my conscience begins,
That your Reverence should have any hand in *my* sins.
So you'd better suppose I committed them all—
For whether they're great ones, or whether they're small,
Or if they're a dozen, or if they're four-score,
'Tis your Reverence knows how to absolve them, asthore:
So, I'll say, in a word, I'm no very good boy,
And, therefore, your blessin', sweet Father Molloy."

" Well," says Father Molloy, " if your sins I forgive,
   So you must forgive all your enemies truly,
And promise me also that, if you should live,
   You'll leave off your old tricks, and begin to live newly."
" I forgive ev'rybody," says Pat, with a groan,
" Except that big vagabone, Micky Malone;
And him I will murdher if ever I can—"
" Tut, tut !" says the priest, " you're a very bad man;

For without your forgiveness, and also repentance,
You'll ne'er go to heaven, and that is my sentence."
" Pooh !" says Paddy McCabe, " that's a very hard case ;
With your Reverence and heaven I'm content to make pace ;
But with heaven and your Reverence I woudher—*och hone*,
You would think of comparin' that blackguard, Malone.
But since I'm hard press'd and that I *must* forgive,
I forgive—if I die ; but as sure as I live
That ugly blackguard I will surely desthroy !—
So *now* for your blessin', sweet Father Molloy !"

PAT'S LETTER.

Well, Mary, me darlint, I'm landed at last,
And troth, though they tell me the st'amer was fast,
It sames as if years upon years had gone by
Since Paddy looked intill yer beautiful eye !
For Amerikay, darlint—ye'll think it is quare—
Is twinty times furder than Cork from Kildare ;
And the say is that broad, and the waves are that high,
Ye're tossed like a fut-ball 'twixt wather and shky ;
And ye fale like a pratie just burstin' the shkin,
That all ye can do is to howld yersilf in.
Ochone ! but, me jewel, the say may be grand :
But, when ye come over, dear, *travel by land !*

It's a wondherful counthry, this—so I am towld—
They'll not look at guineas, so chape is the gowld :
And the three that poor mother sewed into my coat
I sowld for a thrifle, on l'aving the boat.
And the quarest of fashions ye iver have seen !
They pay ye with picters all painted in green.
And the crowds that are rushing here, morning and night,
Would make the lord-lieutenant shake with the fright.
The strates are that full that there's no one can pass,
And the only law is, " Do not thread on the grass."
Their grass is the quarest of shows—by me vow—
For it wouldn't be munched by a Candlemas cow.
Tell father I wint, as he bid me, to see

His friend, Tim O'Shannon, from Killycaughnee.
It's rowling in riches O'Shannon is now,
With a wife and tin babies, six pigs and a cow,
In a nate little house, standing down from the strate,
With two beautiful rooms, and a pig-sty complate.
I thought of ye, darlint, and dramed such a drame!
That mebbe, some day, we'd be living the same;
Though, troth, Tim O'Shannon's wife niver could dare
(Poor yaller-skinned crayther) with you to compare;
While, as for the pigs, shure 'twas aisy to see
The bastes were not mint for this land of the free.

I think of ye, darlint, from morning till night;
And when I'm not thinking ye're still in me sight!
I see your blue eyes, with the sun in their glance—
Your smile in the meadow, your fut in the dance.
I'll love ye, and thrust ye, both living and dead!
(Let Phil Blake look out for his carroty head!)
I'm working, acushla, for you—only you!
And I'll make ye a lady yit, if ye'll be true;
Though, troth, ye can't climb Fortune's laddher so quick,
Whin both of your shouldhers are loaded with brick;
But I'll do it—I declare it, by—this and by that—
Which manes what I daren't say—from

Your own   PAT.

THE BIRTH OF ST. PATRICK.

SAMUEL LOVER.

On the eighth day of March it was, some people say,
That Saint Pathrick at midnight he first saw the day;
While others declare 'twas the ninth he was born,
And 'twas all a mistake between midnight and morn;
For mistakes *will* occur in a hurry and shock,
And some blam'd the babby—and some blam'd the clock—
Till with all their cross-questions sure no one could know
If the child was too fast—or the clock was too slow.

Now the first faction fight in owld Ireland, they say,
Was all on account of Saint Pathrick's birthday;
Some fought for the eighth—for the ninth more would die,

And who wouldn't see right, sure they blacken'd his eye!
At last both the factions so positive grew,
That *each* kept a birthday, so Pat then had *two*,
Till Father Mulcahy, who showed them their sins,
Said, "No one could have two birthdays, but a *twins*."
Says he, "Boys, don't be fightin' for eight or for nine,
Don't be always dividin'—but sometimes combine;
Combine eight with nine, and seventeen is the mark,
So let that be his birthday." "Amen," says the clerk.
"If he wasn't a *twins*, sure our hist'ry will show
That, at least, he's worth any *two* saints that we know!"
Then they all got blind dhrunk—which complated their bliss,
And we keep up the practice from that day to this.

BRIDGET O'HOOLEGOIN'S LETTER.

Tullymucclescrag, Parrish of Ballyraggett, near
Ballysluggathey, County of Kilkenny,
Ireland, Jinuary the 1th.

My DEAR NEPHEW: I haven't sent ye a letther since
the last time I wrote to ye, bekase we have moved from
our former place of livin' and I didn't know where a letther
would find ye; but I now with pleasure take up me pin
to inform ye of the death of yer own livin' unclo, Ned Fitz-
patrick, who died very suddenly a few days ago afther a
lingerin' illness of six weeks. The poor fellow was in
violent convulsions the whole time of his sickness, lyin'
perfectly quiet, and intirely speechless—all the while talkin' incoherently, and cryin' for wather. I had no oppor-
tunity of informin' ye of his death sooner, except I wrote
to ye by the last post, which same went off two days before he died; and then ye would have postage to pay.
I'm at a loss to tell what his death was occasioned by, but
I fear it was by his last sickness, for he was niver well ten
days togither durin' the whole of his confinement; and I
believe his death was brought about by his aitin' too much
of rabbit stuffed with pais and gravy, or pais and gravy

stuffed with rabbit; but be that as it may, when he brathed his last, the docther gave up all hope of his recovery. I needn't tell ye anything about his age, for ye well know that in June next he would have been just seventy-five years old lackin' ten months, and, had he lived till that time, would have been just six months dead. His property now devolves to his next of kin, which all died some time ago, so that I expect it will be divided between us; and ye know his property, which was very large, was sold to pay his debts, and the remainder he lost at a horse-race; but it was the opinion of iverybody at the time he would have won the race, if the baste he run aginst hadn't been too fast for him.

I niver saw a man in all my life, and the docthers all said so, that observed directions or took medicine betther than he did. He said he would as leve dhrink bitter as sweet if it had only the same taste, and ipecakana as wisky punch, if it would only put him in the same humor for fightin'. But, poor sowl! he will niver ate or dhrink any more, and ye haven't a livin' relation in the world except meself and yer two cousins who were kilt in the last war. I cannot dwell on the mournful subject any longer, and shall sale me letther with black salin'-wax, and put in it yer uncle's coat-of-arms. So I beg ye not to brake the sale when ye open the letther, and don't open it until two or three days afther ye resave this, and by that time ye will be well prepared for the sorrowful tidings. Yer old sweetheart sinds her love unknownst to ye. When Jarry McGhee arrives in America, ax him for this letther, and if he don't brung it from amongst the rest, tell him it's the one that spakes about yer uncle's death, and saled in black.

I remain yer affectionate ould grandmother,

BRIDGET O'HOOLEGOIN.

P. S.—Don't write till ye resave this.

N. B.—When yez come to this place, stop, and don't rade any more until my next.

PADDY FAGAN'S PEDIGREE.

Air—"Sprig of Shillaleh."

I'm a tight Irish boy, and from Dublin I came,
I am highly connected, Pat Fagan's my name,
And it isn't meself that's a vulgar spalpeen;
I am all the way there, and in truth, sirs, you'll find
While I'm going ahead, sure I'm never behind;
I never use blarney wid age or wid youth—
If I tell lies all day, sure every word's truth,
    Wid my double-milled larning, and shamrock so green.

SPOKEN.—And where did I larn it all? Sure from the
mother-tongue of my father, who was a fine, motherly man,
but he had a knack of growing, and he'd never lave it off;
from a boy he grew into a young man, then he'd not lave it
off; from a young man he grew into an old man, then he'd
not lave it off; so for a change he grew dead one day, and
then he'd not lave it off, for he grew musty, and fusty, and
rusty; so to keep him sweet above ground we put him under it, and by the powers he'd not lave off growing then,
for the last time we dug him up he wasn't there, for he had
grown himself to waste. Och! but he had a knack of getting over the boys and girls too, for on his table was larning
and potatoes at the same time, and you were welcome to
eat them all and leave the rest behind you. Och! sure he
had a most illigant brogue, and he laid his blarney on with
a trowel, and this was the way of him: "Och!" said he,
"honor your fathers and mothers all the days of their lives,
if they died before you were born. Keep your hands from
picking and stealing, or if you steal anything mind it belongs to yoursilf. Niver spake ill of your neighbor widout
giving him a good character. Keep your tongue from lying and slandering, unless you speak thruth all the time
you are doing of it. Niver break your word widout keeping
of it at the same time. Always honestly pay your debts
whether you owe any or not. Niver borrow an article of a
neighbor that he has not got to lend you, or you are likely

to get disappointed; by the same rule niver lind an article that you have not got; if you do, you will never get it back again. Niver try to keep an empty sieve full of water, or attempt to bottle off the wind, or run afther a flash of lightning. But there are some people who are so disagreeable, that they are niver quiet but when they are kicking up a row, and niver satisfied but when they are discontinted. Now such people should go to some uninhabited, unknown country which they can't find out, and not let their frinds know where to find them. Thin when they were all alone, like Adam and Eve were in the garden of St. Stephen, if they should have a row wid their next-door neighbor, to save peace and quietness, and prevent blows, box it out wid them." This is the way me father taught me, and thus I lead his way while he goes before me.

I'm a tight Irish boy, etc.

PAT O'FLANIGAN'S COLT.

An Irish Recitation.

Patrick O'Flanigan, from Erin's isle
Just fresh, thinking he'd walk around a while,
With open mouth and widely staring eyes,
Cried " Och !" and " Whist !" at every new surprise.
He saw some laborers in a field of corn ;
The golden pumpkins lit the scene with glory ;
Of all that he had heard since being born,
Nothing had equaled this in song or story.
" The holy mither ! and, sirs, would ye plaise
To be a tellin' me what might be these ?
An' sure I'm thinkin' that they're not pratees,
But maybe it's the way you grow your chase."
" Ah, Patrick, these are mare's eggs," said the hand,
Giving a wink to John, and Jim, and Bill ;
" Just hatch it out, and then you have your horse ;
Take one and try it ; it will pay you well."

" Faith an' that's aisy sure ; in dear ould Ireland
  I always had my Christmas pig so nate,
  Fatted on buttermilk, and hard to bate ;
  But only gintlemen can own a horse.
  Ameriky's a great counthry indade ;
  I thought that here I'd kape a pig, of coorse,
  Have me own land, and shanty without rent,
  An' have me vote, an' taxes not a cint ;
  But sure I niver thought to own a baste.
  An' won't the wife and childer now be glad ?
  A thousand blissings on your honor's head !
  But could ye tell by lookin' at the egg
  What color it will hatch ? It's to me taste
  To have a dapple gray, with a long tail,
  High in the neck, and slinder in the leg,
  To jump a twel' feet bog, and niver fail,
  Like me Lord Dumferline's at last year's races—"
Just then the merry look on all their faces
Checked Patrick's flow of talk, and with a blush
That swept his face as milk goes over mush,
He added, " Sure, I know it is no use
To try to tell by peering at an egg
If it will hatch a gander or a goose ;"
Then looked around to make judicious choice.
" Pick out the largest one that you can hide
  Out of the owner's sight there by the river ;
  Don't drop and break it, or the colt is gone ;
  Carry it gently to your little farm,
  Put it in bed, and keep it six weeks warm."
  Quickly Pat seized a huge, ripe, yellow one,
" Faith, sure, an I'll do every bit of that.
  The whole sax wakes I'll lie meself in bed,
  An' keep it warrum, as your honor said ;
  Long life to yees, and may you niver walk,
  Not even to your grave, but ride foriver ;
  Good luck to yees," and without more of talk
He pulled the forelock neath his tattered hat,
And started off ; but plans of mice and men
Gang oft agley, again and yet again.

Full half a mile upon his homeward road
Poor Patrick toiled beneath his heavy load.
A hilltop gained, he stopped to rest, alas!
He laid his mare's egg on some treacherous grass;
When down the steep hillside it rolled away,
And at poor Patrick's call made no delay.
Gaining momentum, with a heavy thump,
It struck and split upon a hollow stump,
In which a rabbit lived with child and wife.
Frightened, the timid creature ran for life.
" Shtop, shtop my colt!" cried Patrick, as he ran
After his straying colt, but all in vain.
With ears erect poor Bunny faster fled
As " Shtop my colt!" in mournful, eager tones
Struck on those organs, till with fright half dead
He hid away among some grass and stones.
Here Patrick searched till rose the harvest moon,
Braying and whinnying till he was hoarse,
Hoping to lure the colt by this fond cheat;
" For won't the young thing want his mither soon,
And come to take a bit of something t' eat ?"
But vain the tender accents of his call—
No colt responded from the broken wall;
And 'neath the twinkling stars he plodded on,
To tell how he had got and lost his horse.
" As swate a gray as iver eyes sat on,"
He said to Bridget and the children eight,
After thrice telling the whole story o'er;
" The way he run it would be hard to bate;
So little, too, with jist a whisk o' tail,
Not a pin-feather on it as I could see,
For it was hatched out just sax weeks too soon!
An' such long ears were niver grown before
On any donkey in grane Ireland!
So little, too, you'd hold it in your hand;
Och hone! he would have made a gay donkey."
So all the sad O Flanigans that night
Held a loud wake over the donkey gone,
Eating their " praties " without milk or salt,

Howling between whiles, " Och ! my little colt !"
While Bunny, trembling from his dreadful fright,
Skipped home to Mrs. B. by light of moon,
And told the story of his scare and flight ;
And all the neighboring rabbits played around
The broken mare's egg scattered on the ground.

PAT AND THE OYSTERS.

One evening a red-headed Connaught swell, of no small
aristocratic pretensions in his own eyes, sent his servant,
whom he had just imported from the long-horned kingdom,
in all the rough majesty of a creature fresh from the
" wilds," to purchase a hundred of oysters on the City
Quay. Paddy staid so long away, that Squire Trigger got
quite impatient and unhappy, lest his " body man" might
have slipped into the Liffey. However, to his infinite re-
lief, Paddy soon made his appearance, puffing and blowing
like a disabled bellows, but carrying his load seemingly in
great triumph. " Well, Pat," cried the master, "what
the devil kept you so long ?" " Long ! Ah, thin, maybe
it's what you'd have me to come home with half my *arrant?"*
says Pat. " Half the oysters ?" says the master. " No ;
but too much of the *fish*," says Pat. " What fish ?" says
he. " The oysters, to be sure," says Pat. " What do you
mean, blockhead ?" says he. " I mean," says Pat, " that
there was no use in loading myself with more nor was useful." " Will you explain yourself?" says he. " I will,"
says Pat, laying down his load. " Well, then, you see,
plaise your honor, as I was coming home along the quay,
mighty peaceable, who should I meet but Shammus
Maginus ? ' Good-morrow, Shamien,' sis I. ' Good mor-
row, kindly, Paudeen,' sis he. ' What is it you have in the
sack ?' sis he. ' A hundred of oysters,' sis I. ' Let us look
at them,' sis he. ' I will, and welcome,' sis I. 'Arrah !

thunder and pratees!' sis he, opening the sack, and examinin' them, 'who *sowld* you these?' 'One Tom Kinahan that keeps a small ship there below,' sis I. 'Musha, then, bad luck to that same Tom that *sowld* the likes to you!' sis he. 'Arrah! why, avick?' sis I. 'To make a *bolsour* ov you, an' give them to you without claning thim,' sis he. 'An' arn't they claned, Jim, aroon?' sis I. 'Oh! bad luck to the one of thim,' sis he. 'Musha then,' says I, 'what the dhoul will I do at all, at all? for the master will be mad.' 'Do!' sis he, 'why, I'd rather do the thing for you myself, nor you should lose your place,' sis he. So wid that he begins to clane them with his knife, *nate* and *well*, an', afeered ov dirtying the flags, begor, he swallowed the insides himself from beginnin' to ind, tal he had them as dacent as you see thim here," dashing down at his master's feet his bag of oyster-shells, to his master's no small amazement.

JIMMY McBRIDE'S LETTER.

The following characteristic letter was written by a Hibernian, after six years' experience of American institutions:

New York, Dec. the one, 1867.

My dear Mary, the darlint of my heart and sowl, I am well, but had the favor and ague; and I hope you are in the same condition, thanks be to God. I wish you many happy New Years, and the childer, and hope you will have threescore and ten of them. We had a Christmas here, But the Haythens don't keep it like we used at home. Divil resave the one ivir said to me Many Happy Christmas, or Bad luck to you, or any other Politeness. I did not get a Christmas box until i was going home that night, and a night-walking Blackguard gave me one on the eye, and axed me for my money. I gave him all i could, about a score of pounds, which knocked the sinse out of him. Dear Mary, They tell me that the Nagur is going to be the White Man in future; and the White Nagurs in Congress, a public house in Washington, are going to try the President for being a white man. If they find him guilty, and there is no doubt of it, for they are accusers, witnesses, lawyers and judges all in one, they are going to execute him, make a fellow called Coldfacks President, and remove the state of Government to a place called Boshton, celebrated for its republicans and sinners. Thim is the same as the Rediculous fellows they call Ridicules, or Radicals, saving your Prisence. They want to continue their own Power, God Betune us and all harm. They say the Southerners must go down on their knees to them. They forget that the poor divils are flat on their backs already; and they are a mane set to kick a man whin he's down. Be jabers it makes my Blood bile to think of it. One war is no sooner inded then they Commence the begining of another in Washington; an' God knows whin or where it may ind. I lost one fine leg in the last, But i have another left for a good cause, and I'll fight for Johnson, for i hear his Great Grandmother, by his forefather's side, was an Irishman. We have snow and frost here, and is likely to have more weather. The temperance men, God save the mark, in a place called Albany, where the people sind ripresentatives to chate thim, have stopt our grog, only By Daylight. Divil a much matter anyways, for they don't kape a dacint drap of drink in the country; no raal ould Irish Poteen; nothing but stuff that would kill a pig, if he had to live on it, much less a Christian Baste.

Remember me to Darby. Tell him he's well, and ax him how i am. I am sorry to hear of the death of the Bull, and hope you are likewise; her milk is a loss. Tell Teddy McFinn if he comes out here he will see more of

America in one day than if he staid home all his life. I am glad his wife got over the twins, and hope she'll do better the next time, there is room for improvement. I like this country; but there is no place like ould Ireland, where you'd get as much whisky for a shilling as would make tay for six people. If you get this, write soon; if you don't, write and let me know. I may be dead, for life is uncertain under the Radicals. But dead or alive I'll answer your letter. Address your dear Brother Jimmy, New York, America.

JIMMY MC BRIDE.

PADDY McGRATH'S INTRODUCTION TO MR. BRUIN.

An Irish Story.

Not long since I was walking with Jimmy Butler through a thick wood on me way to Judy O'Flinn's, to pay me bist addrissis to her, whin Jimmy very suddintly cried out, "Be jabers! but there's Mr. Bruin!" and with that he runs off like a shot, lavin' me alone jist forninst the ould gintleman.

"Mr. Bruin, are ye?" says I. "How do you do, Mr. Bruin? Happy to know yer worship, and hope yer honor's well. Happy o' yer acquaintance," says I. A grunt was the only answer I resaved.

"Och, sure!" thinks I, "yer a quare ould chap at iny rate;" and thin I axed him how Mrs. Bruin and all the young spalpeen Bruins prospered. He only gev me another grunt. "Bad luck to yer eddication!" says I. "Where did ye hev yer bringin' up? Me name's Paddy McGrath, of Tipperary county, ould Ireland, at yer sarvice," says I agin, thinkin' to hev some conversation wid him. He only showed me his big grinders and gev me another grunt, but he still stood lookin' at me. "Be dad! but he's niver been taught his letthers, and cannot understhand me, or

his eyes must be mighty wake and bad. The top o' the
mornin' to yez ? Do yez always wear yer coat with the wool
on the outside ?" says I agin.

This samed to touch a tinder pint wid him, and he kem
towards me. Holdin' out me hand, I wint to mate him.
" Excuse the complimint," says I, " but you've a mighty
oogly moog, so ye hev."

He grinned mighty plazed like, and held out his arrums
to embrace me. Jist as I kem widin rache of his long
arrums, he gev me a cuff aside me hid, which sint me flyin'.
Me sinsis lift me mighty quick afther he sthruck me, and
whin they kem back, I found mesel' a-rollin' down a shtape
hill, wid no chance to sthop. Prisintly, howiver, I sthruck
a big stoomp, and suddintly sthopped. Whin I got on me
fate agin, I saw Mr. Bruin comin' afther me on his hands
and knase, and grinnin' as much as to say, " I beg yer
pardin, but I didn't mane to tip yez so hard."

" Och, I furgive yez," says I: " come to me arrums,
Mr. Bruin. Paddy McGrath is not the filler to hould a
groodge agin a friud. Yer as welcome to me embrace as
me own Judy." This samed to plaze the ould gint mightily, for he shtood on his fate and agin held out his arrums;
I rushed to his embrace widout another word.

" Och, murdher! murdher!" I scramed; "yer a practiced
hugger, ye are! ye've been in the business afore! How
I pity Mrs. Bruin if ye sarve her this way often. Och,
murdher!" I cried agin; " I don't like such tight squazin'.
I'll be satisfied wid the little ye've gev me if ye'll loosen
yer howld, and gev me a rist."

He gev me a harder squaze than iver, and opened his
big oogly jaws and tried to bite me nose off.

" Bedad! are ye a haythen cannibal?" says I, " that
ye'd take a filler's hid off to show yer love for him?"

He gev me another hug, and fastened his big taath onto
me lift shoulder. " Bad cess to ye!" says I, " but yer
afther makin' too fra wid me on short acquaintince; but

I'll be aven wid yez ;" so sayin', I twisted me arrum from his grasp, and, thrustin' me shillaly into his mouth, gev it a twist with such mighty force that I broke his under jaw.

The ould gint samed to think he had been too lovin' wid me, so givin' a grunt, he let go me shoulder, takin' a pound of me tinder flish wid him, which he ate with a big relish.

" Bedad ! Paddy ! if yez don't outdo yer new friend, he'll lave but little of yez for yer Judy," thinks I, and widout more ado I gev him a blow between his eyes. He gev a quick jerk back, and I sprang from his embrace—but, och ! deary me ! he took the whole of me fine coat, weskit, and shirt but the shlaves, and started off wid 'em. " Och ! ye thavin' murdherin' nager," says I, " bring back me close or I can't pay me addrissis to me Judy, darlint."

He niver paid me a bit o' notice, but rooshed off. I stharted afther the haythenish baste.

He climbed up a big tra mighty quick, takin' me close wid him. I axed him, very perlite like, to throw down me wearin' apparel, but he only blinked his bloody eyes at me.

I was jist goin' to throw me shillaly at him, when I heard a gun go off, and Mr. Bruin gev a terrible squail, dhropped me close, and kem toomblin' to the ground. I looked around in astonishment, and saw Jimmy Butler and siveral others, comin' down the hill towards me.

Whin Jimmy saw me alive he cried like a spalpeen, and rushed into me arrums. When he let me go, I axed him what he mint by shootin' Mr. Bruin in that way. He told me he was a bear and would hev kilt me. "A bear ! did ye say !" says I, " why didn't yez tell me afore so that I could hev kipt ye company in yer runnin' away from him ? A bear !" says I, agin, beginnin' to trimble for fear the ould gint might not be quite dead—" give him another shot, Jimmy, to be sure ye've kilt him intirely."

He was dead sure enough, and we lift him alone quite gory.

Jimmy got me some new close, and we wint home.

Whin I told Judy of the squazin' I got, she blushed, and put her arrums around me nick, and gev me so soft a squaze that, for a time, I forgot me introduction to Mr. Bruin.

MR. O'HOOLAHAN'S MISTAKE.

An Irish Recitation.

An amusing scene occurred in Justice Young's court-room an evening or two since. Two sons of the "ould sod," full of "chain-lightning" and law, rushed in, and, advancing to the justice's little law-pulpit at the rear of the court-room, both began talking at once.

"One at a time, if you please," said the judge.

"Judge—yer—honor—will I sphake thin?" said one of the men.

"Silence!" roared his companion. "I am here! Let me talk! Phwat do you know about law?"

"Keep still yourself, sir," said the judge. "Let him say what he wants."

"Well, I want me naime aff the paiper. That's phwat I want," said the man.

"Off what paper?" said the judge.

"Well, aff the paiper: ye ought to know what paiper. Sure, ye married me, they say."

"To whom?" asked the judge.

"Some female, sir; and I don't want her, sir. It don't go! and I want me naime aff the paiper."

"Silence!" roared the friend, bringing his huge fist down upon the little pulpit, just under the judge's nose, with a tremendous thwack. "Silence! I am here. Phwat do you know about law? Sure, yer honor, it was Tim McCloskey's wife that he married—his widdy, I mane. You married thim, yer honor."

"And I was dhrunk at the time, sir. Yis, sir; and I was not a free aigent; an' I don't know a thing about it, sir—do you see? I want me naime aff the paiper—I repudiate, sir."

"Silence! Let me spake. Phwat do you know about law?" bringing his fist down upon the judge's desk.

"But I was dhrunk: I was not at the time a free aigent."

"Silence! I am here to spake. It does not depind on that at all. It depinds—and there is the whole pint, both in law and equity—it depinds whether was the woman a sole thrader or not at the time this marriage was solemnated. That is the pint, both in law and equity!"

"But I was dhrunk at the time. Divil roawst me if I knowed I was gittin' married. I was not a free aigent. I want the judge to taik me naime aff the paiper. It don't go."

The judge tried to explain to the man that, drunk or sober, he was married to the woman fast enough, and, if he wanted a divorce, he must go to another court.

"Burn me up!" cried the man, "if I go to another court. Ye married me, and ye can unmarry me. Taik me naime aff the paiper!"

"Silence!" cried the friend, bringing his fist down in close proximity to the judge's nose. "Phwat do you know about law? I admit, judge, that he must go to a higher court; that is (down comes the fist) if the woman can prove (whack) that she was at the time the marriage was solemnated (whack) a regularly ordained sole thrader (whack). On this pint it depinds, both in law and equity."

"I have had enough of this!" cried the judge: "I cannot divorce you. You are married, and married you must remain, for all I can do."

"Ye won't taik me naime aff the paiper, thin!"

"It would not mend the matter," said the judge.

"Ye won't taik it aff?"

"No: I won't!" fairly yelled the judge.

"Silence!" cried the partner, bringing down his fist, and

raising a cloud of dust under the judge's nose. "It depinds whether, at the time, the woman was a regular sole—"

"Get out of here," cried the judge. "I've had about enough of this!" at the same time rising.

"Ye won't taik it aff? Very well, thin, I'll go hoam and devorce myself. I'll fire the thatch! I will—"

Here he glanced toward the front door: his under jaw drooped, he ceased speaking, and in a half-stooping posture he went out of the back door of the office like a shot.

The valiant friend and legal adviser also glanced toward the door, when he, too, doubled up and *scooted* in the footsteps of his illustrious principal.

A look at the door showed it darkened by a woman about six feet in height, and so broad as to fill it almost from side to side.

The judge took a look at this mountain of flesh, doubled up, and was about to take the back track, but thought better of it, and took refuge behind his little law-pulpit.

The mountain advanced, gave utterance in a sort of internal rumble, and then, amid fire, smoke, and burning lava, belched out—

"Did I, or did I not see Michael O'Hoolahan sneak out of your back doore?"

"I believe O'Hoolahan is the name of one of the gentlemen who just went out," said the judge.

Advancing upon the pulpit, behind which the judge settled lower and lower, the mountain belched,—

"You be-e-lave! You *know* it was Michael O'Hoolahan! Now, what is all this connivin' in here about? Am I a widdy agin? Did ye taik his naime aff the paiper? Did ye taik it aff?"

"N-no," said the judge.

"Ye didn't? Don't ye desave me!"

"No: I give you my word of honor I didn't, couldn't—I had no right."

"It's well for ye ye didn't. I'll tache him to be rinnin'

about connivin' to lave me a lone widdy agin', whin I'm
makin' a jintleman of him!"

"With this she sailed back to the door, where she turned,
and, shaking her fist, thus addressed the tip of the judge's
nose, which alone was visible above the little pulpit,—

"Now, do you mind that ye lave his naime on the paiper!
I want no meddlin' wid a man wanst I git him. No more
connivin'!"

KITTY MALONE.

KATE TRUE.

"It's tellin' my story, ye're askin'?
  Shure, miss, there is little to tell;
The children are down with the fayver,
  And mesilf, I am not over well.

"Where's Pat? Shure, now, ye are taysin';
  Who knows, when a man is away?
The woman must bide with the babbies,
  And niver be idle nor play.

"Out of work? Shure ye are right, miss,
  Not a ha'porth he's done for a year.
Git along, is it? Why, 'tis the washin'
  And scrubbin' that kapes us all here.

"Ye see, miss, when Pat is a-slaypin'
  So swate, and a-dramin' of heaven,
Why, I tend the babbies and washes
  For you folks in two twenty-seven.

"And thin I'll be mindin' the childer,
  The fayver is hard on 'em, dear—
What's ailin' the likes of ye, lady?
  Yer swate eyes is wet wid a tear!

"Ye see, as I said, while Pat's slaypin',
  I'm airning our pennies for bread,
Or givin' a sup to poor Johnnie,
  Or puttin' the babby to bed.

"It keeps me that busy, I never
  Know whether it rains or it snows.
Quit washin'? Why, bless ye, dear lady,
  These poor little lambs would be froze.

"And Pat is that fond of me, lady,
  'Twould make ye to smile, could ye see
How he'll coax for a bit of terbaccy,
  And hangs round the likes of poor me.

"Make him work? Now, my lady, ye're foolin'—
  Do ye think he could stand at the tub,
And wring out the close for the gentry?
  Or go down on his knees for to scrub?

"Pat's a mighty fine man, thin, my lady.
  Does he drink? Shure, niver a drop;
He is aisy, my Pat, an' he tells me,
  'Shure, Kit, you will never give up.'

"And no more will I thin, while my babbies
  Creep round on this old cabin floor;
And Pat, he jist smokes, so continted,
  And throws me a smack at the door.

"Down-hearted? Oh, bless ye, swate lady,
  There's times when I can't spake a prayer—
The babbies, mayhap, wantin' breakfast,
  And me not a crust for the pair;

"Or the meal, maybe, gone from the cupboard,
  Or the landlord has asked for his rint;
Oh, my heart goes down like a stone, miss,
  And me not ownin' a cint.

"And Pat? Oh, he jist goes away thin—
  Men cannot bide trouble at home—
And I? Well, dear, Kitty McCarthy
  Was gayer nor Kitty Malone."

      *   *   *   *   *   *

Oh, tender and true-hearted Womanhood,
  Whether found in palace or cot,
What knows the world of thy virtues?
  How soon thy toil is forgot!

On the roll of the army of martyrs
    Write a name—on a pure white stone;
Only God and the angels know thee,
    Poor, battle-scarred Kitty Malone!

IRISH ASTRONOMY.

CHARLES G. HALPINE.

A veritable myth, touching the constellation of O'RYAN, ignorantly and falsely spelled ORION.

O'Ryan was a man of might,
    Whin Ireland was a nation,
But poachin' was his heart's delight,
    And constant occupation.
He had an ould militia gun,
    And sartin sure his aim was;
He gave the keepers many a run,
    And wouldn't mind the game laws.

St. Pathrick wanst was passin' by
    O'Ryan's little houldin',
And as the saint felt wake and dhry,
    He thought he'd enther bould in;
"O'Ryan," says the saint, "avick!
    To praich at Thurles I'm goin';
So let me have a rasher, quick,
    And a dhrop of Innishowen."

"No rasher will I cook for you
    While betther is to spare, sir;
But here's a jug of mountain dew,
    And there's a rattlin' hare, sir."
St. Pathrick he look'd mighty sweet,
    And says he "Good luck attind you,
And when you're in your windin' sheet
    It's up to heaven I'll sind you."

O'Ryan gave his pipe a whiff—
    "Them tidin's is thransportin',
But may I ax your saintship if
    There's any kind of sportin'?"

St. Pathrick said, " A Lion's there,
   Two Bears, a Bull, and Cancer"—
" Bedad," says Mick, " the huntin's rare,
   St. Pathrick, I'm your man, sir !"

So, to conclude my song aright,
   For fear I'd tire your patience,
You'll see O'Ryan any night
   Amid the constellations.
And Venus follows in his track,
   Till Mars grows jealous raally,
But, faith, he fears the Irish knack
   Of handling his shillaly.

PATRICK O'ROUKE AND THE FROGS.

GEORGE W. BUNGAY.

Saint Patrick did a vast deal of good in his day ; he not only drove the snakes out of Ireland, but he also drove away the frogs—at least I judge so from the fact that Patrick O'-Rouke was unfamiliar with the voices of these noisy hydropaths.   Pat had been visiting at the house of a friend, and he had unfortunately imbibed more whisky than ordinary mortals can absorb with safety to their persons.   On his return home the road was too narrow, and he performed wonderful feats in his endeavors to maintain the centre of gravity.   Now he seemed to exert his best efforts to walk on both sides of the road at the same time ; then he would fall and feel upward for the ground ; then he would slowly pick himself up, and the ground would rise and hit him square in the face.   By the time he reached the meadowlands, located about half-way betwixt his home and the shanty of his friend, he was somewhat sobered by the ups and downs he had experienced on the way.

Hearing strange voices, he stopped suddenly to ascertain if possible the purport of their language.   Judge his astonishment when he heard his own name distinctly called, " Patrick O'Rouke—Patrick O'Rouke."

" Faith, that's me name, sure."

"Patrick O'Rouke—Patrick—O'Rouke—Rouke—Rouke."

" What do ye want o' the likes o' me ?" he inquired.

" When did you come over—come over—come over ?"

" It is jest tree months ago to the minute, and a bad time we had, sure, for we wur all say-sick, and the passage lasted six long wakes."

" What will you do—do—do ? What will you do—do —do ?"

" I have nothing to do at all at all; but then I can do anything: I can dig; I can tind mason; and I can hould office, if I can git it."

" You are drunk—you are drunk—drunk—drunk—drunk —drunk."

" By my soul that's a lie."

" You are drunk—dead drunk—drunk—drunk."

" Repate that same if ye dare and I will take me shillaly to ye."

" You are drunk—dead drunk—drunk—drunk."

" Jist come out here now and stip on the tail o' me coat, like a man," exclaimed Pat in high dudgeon, pulling off his coat and trailing it upon the ground.

" Strike him—strike him—strike—strike—strike."

" Come on wid ye, and the divil take the hindmost · I am a broth of a boy—come on."

" Knock him down—down—down."

" I will take any one in the crowd, and if Mike Mulligan was here we would take all of yees at onct."

" Kill him—kill him—kill him."

" Och, murther! sure ye wud not be afther murdering me—I was not oncivil to ye. Go back to Pate Dogan's wid me now, and I will trate ivery one of yees."

" We don't drink rum—rum—rum."

" And are ye all Father Matthew men ?"

" We are cold watermen—watermen."

" Take me advice now, and put a little whasky in the

wather, darlings : it will kape the cowld out whin yees git
wet, and so it will."

" Moderation—moderation—moderation."

" Yis, that's the talk.   I wint to Pate Dogan's, down
there in Brownville, and says I, ' Will ye stand trate ?'
Says he, ' Faith, and I will.'   Says I, ' Fill up the glass ;'
and so he did ; ' Fill it agin,' said I, and so he did ; ' and
agin,' said I, and so he did.   ' Give me the bottle,' said I.
'And I won't do that same,' said he.   ' Give me the bottle,'
said I, and he kipt on niver heedin' me at all at all, so I
struck him wid me fist rite in his partatee thrap, and he
kicked me out o' the house, and I took the hint that he
didn't want me there, so I lift."

" Blackguard and bully—blackguard and bully."

" Ye wouldn't dare say that to my face in broad day,
sure ; but ye are a set of futpads and highwaymin, hiding
behind the rocks and the traas.   Win I onct git to Watertown
I will sind Father Fairbanks afther ye, and he will chuck
ye into the pond as he did that thafe who stole the public
money, and he will hould ye there until ye confess, or he
will take yees to the perleese."

" Come on, boys—chase him—chase him."

" Faith, and I won't run, but I will jist walk rite along,
for if any of me frinds shud find me here in sich company,
at this time o' night, they wud think I was thrying for to
stale somethin'.   Tak me advice, boys, and go home, for
it's goin' for to rain, and ye will git wet to the skin if ye
kape sich late hours."

" Catch him—catch him—catch him."

" Sure ye'd bether not, for I haven't got a cint wid me or
I'd lave it in yer jackets.   What's the use of staling all a
man has whin he has jist nothing at all at all ?   Bad luck
. to ye for bothering me so."

About this time the frog concert was in full tune, and the
hoarse chorus so alarmed Pat that he took to his heels, for
he was now sober enough to run.   Reaching his home, two

miles distant from the scene of his encounter with the "high-waymin" who held such a long parley with him, he gave a graphic history of his grievance. Soon it was noised about the neighborhood that Patrick O'Rouke had been waylaid and abused by a drunken set of vagabonds, whose head-quarters were near a meadow on the banks of the Black River; but the fear of the citizens subsided when they discovered that Pat had been out on a bender, and could not distinguish a frog from a friend or an enemy.

IRISH COQUETRY.

Says Patrick to Biddy, "Good-mornin', me dear!
It's a bit av a sacret I've got for yer ear:
It's yoursel' that is lukin' so charmin' the day,
That the heart in me breast is fast slippin' away."
" 'Tis you that kin flatther," Miss Biddy replies,
And throws him a glance from her merry blue eyes.

" Arrah, thin," cries Patrick, " 'tis thinkin' av you
That's makin' me heart-sick, me darlint, that's thrue!
Sure I've waited a long while to tell ye this same,
And Biddy Maloney will be such a foine name."
Cries Biddy, "Have done wid yer talkin,' I pray;
Shure me heart's not me own for this many a day!

" I gave it away to a good-lookin' boy,
Who thinks there is no one like Biddy Malloy;
So don't bother me, Pat; jist be aisy," says she.
" Indade, if ye'll let me, I will that!" says he;
" It's a bit of a flirt that ye are, on the sly;
I'll not trouble ye more, but I'll bid ye good-by."

" Arrah, Patrick," cries Biddy, " an' where are ye goin'?
Sure it isn't the best of good manners ye're showin'
To lave me so suddint!" " Och, Biddy," says Pat,
" You have knocked the cock-feathers jist out av me hat!"
" Come back, Pat!" says she. " What fur, thin?" says he.
" Bekase I meant you all the time, sir!" says she.

KING O'TOOLE AND SAINT KEVIN.

SAMUEL LOVER.

" Well, sir, you must know that there was wanst a king called King O'Toole, who was a fine ould king in the ould ancient times, long ago; and it was him that ownded the Churches in the airly days."

"Surely," said I, "the churches were not in King O'Toole's time?"

" Oh, by no manes, yer honor—troth, it's yourself that's right enough there—but you know the place is called 'The Churches,' bekase they wor built *afther* by Saint Kavin, and wint by the name o' the Churches iver more; and therefore, av coorse, the place bein' so called, I say that the king ownded the Churches—and why not, sir, seein' 'twas his birthright, time out o' mind, beyant the flood? Well, the king, you see, was the right sort—he was the rale boy, and loved sport as he loved his life, and huntin' in partic'lar; and from the rising o' the sun, up he got, and away he wint over the mountains beyant afther the deer : and the fine times them wor ; for the deer was as plinty thin, aye, throth, far plintyer than the sheep is now; and that's the way it was with the king, from the crow o' the cock to the song o' the redbreast.

" In this counthry, sir," added he, speaking parenthetically, in an under-tone, " we think it unlooky to kill the redbreast, for the robin is God's own bird."

Then, elevating his voice to its former pitch, he proceeded :

" Well, it was all mighty good as long as the king had his health ; but, you see, in coorse o' time the king grewn owld, by raison he was stiff in his limbs, and when he got sthricken in years, his heart failed him, and he was lost intirely for want of divarshin, bekase he couldn't go a huntin' no longer, and by dad, the poor king was obleeged at last for to get a goose to divart him."

Here an involuntary smile was produced by this regal mode of recreation, " the royal game of goose."

" Oh, you may laugh, if you like," said he, half affronted, " but it's thruth I'm tellin' you; and the way the goose divarted him was this-a-way : you see, the goose used for to swim acrass the lake, and go down divin' for throut (and not finer throut in all Ireland than the same throut) and cotch fish on a Friday for the king, and flew every other day round about the lake, divartin' the poor king, that you'd think he'd break his sides laughin' at the frolicsome tricks av his goose ; so in coorse o' time the goose was the greatest pet in the counthry, and the biggest rogue, and divarted the king to no end, and the poor king was as happy as the day was long. So that's the way it was ; and all went on mighty well, until, by dad, the goose got sthricken in years, as well as the king, and grewn stiff in the limbs, like her masther, and couldn't divart him no longer ; and then it was that the poor king was lost complate, and didn't know what in the wide world to do, seein' he was done out of all divarshin, by raison that the goose was no more in the flower of her blame.

" Well, the king was nigh hand broken-hearted, and melancholy intirely, and was walkin' one mornin' by the edge of the lake, lamentin' his cruel fate, an' thinkin' o' drownin' himself, that could get no divarshin in life, when all of a suddint, turnin' round the corner beyant, who should he meet but a mighty dacent young man comin' up to him.

" ' God save you,' says the king (for the king was a civil-spoken gintleman, by all accounts), ' God save you,' says he to the young man.

" 'God save you kindly,' says the young man to him back again ; ' God save you,' says he, ' King O'Toole.'

" ' True for you,' says the king, ' I am King O'Toole,' says he, ' prince and plennypennytinchery o' these parts,' says he ; ' but how kem ye to know that ?' says he.

"'Oh, niver mind,' says Saint Kavin.

"For you see," said old Joe, in his under-tone again, and looking very knowingly, "it *was* Saint Kavin, sure enough—the saint himself in disguise, and nobody else. 'Oh, niver mind,' says he, 'I know more than that,' says he, 'nor twice that.'

"'And who are you that makes so bowld—who are you at all at all!'

"'Oh, never you mind,' says Saint Kavin, 'who I am; you'll know more o' me before we part, King O'Toole,' says he.

"'I'll be proud o' the knowledge o' your acquaintance, sir,' says the king, mighty p'lite.

"'Troth, you may say that,' says Saint Kavin. 'And now, may I make bowld to ax, how is your goose, King O'Toole?' says he.

"'Blur-an-agers, how kem you to know about my goose?' says the king.

"'Oh, no matther—I was given to undherstand it,' says Saint Kavin.

"'Oh, that's a folly to talk,' says the king; 'because myself and my goose is private friends,' says he, 'and no one could tell you,' says he, 'barrin' the fairies.'

"'Oh, thin it wasn't the fairies,' says Saint Kavin; 'for I'd have you to know,' says he, 'that I don't keep the likes o' sitch company.'

"'You might do worse, then, my gay fellow,' says the king; 'for it's *they* could show you a crock o' money as aisy as kiss hand; and that's not to be sneezed at,' says the king, 'by a poor man,' says he.

"'Maybe I've a betther way of makin' money myself,' says the saint.

"'By gor,' says the king, 'barrin' you're a coiner,' says he, 'that's impossible!'

"'I'd scorn to be the like, my lord!' says Saint Kavin, mighty high; 'I'd scorn to be the like,' says he.

" 'Then what are you?' says the king, 'that makes money so aisy, by your own account.'

" 'I'm an honest man,' says Saint Kavin.

" 'Well, honest man,' says the king, 'how is it you made your money so aisy?'

" 'By makin' ould things as good as new,' says Saint Kavin.

" 'Blur-an-ouns, is it a tinker you are?' says the king.

" 'No,' says the saint; 'I'm no tinker by thrade, King O'Toole; I've a betther thrade than a tinker,' says he. 'What would you say,' says he, 'if I made your ould goose as good as new?'

"My dear, at the words o' makin' his goose as good as new, you'd think the poor ould king's eyes was ready to jump out iv his head, 'And,' says he—'troth, then, I'd give you more money nor you could count,' says he, 'if you did the like ; and I'd be behoulden to you into the bargain.'

" 'I scorn your dirty money,' says Saint Kavin.

" 'Faith, then, I'm thinkin' a trifle o' change would do you no harm,' says the king, lookin' up sly at the old *caubeen* that Saint Kavin had on him.

" 'I have a vow agin it,' says the saint ; 'and I am book sworn,' says he, 'never to have gold, silver or brass in my company.'

" 'Barrin' the trifle you can't help,' says the king, mighty cute, and looking him straight in the face.

" 'You just hot it,' says Saint Kavin ; 'but though I can't take money,' says he, 'I could take a few acres o' land, if you'd give them to me.'

" 'With all the veins o' my heart,' says the king, 'if you can do what you say.'

" 'Thry me !' says Saint Kavin. 'Call down your goose here,' says he, 'and I'll see what I can do for her.'

"With that the king whistled, and down kem the poor goose, all as one as a hound, waddlin' up to the poor ould cripple, her masther, and as like him as two *pays*. The

minute the saint clapped his eyes an the goose, ' I'll do
the job for you,' says he, ' King O'Toole !'

" ' By *Jaminee*,' says King O'Toole, ' if you do, but I'll
say you are the cleverest fellow in the sivin parishes.'

" ' Och, by dad,' says Saint Kavin, ' you must say more
nor that—my horn's not so soft all out,' says he, ' as to
repair your ould goose for nothin'. What'll you gi' me if
I do the job for you ?—that's the chat,' says Saint Kavin.

" ' I'll give you whatever you ax,' says the king; 'isn't
that fair ?'

" ' Divil a fairer,' says the saint; ' that's the way to do
business. Now,' says he, ' this is a bargain I'll make with
you, King O'Toole: will you gi' me all the ground the goose
flies over, the first offer afther I make her as good as new ?'

" ' I will,' says the king.

" ' You won't go back o' your word ?' says Saint Kavin.

" ' Honor bright !' says King O'Toole, howldin' out his
fist."

Here old Joe, after applying his hand to his mouth, and
making a sharp blowing sound (something like " *thp*,")
extended it to illustrate the action.

" ' Honor bright,' says Saint Kavin back again, ' it's a
bargain,' says he. ' Come here !' says he to the poor old
goose—' come here, you unfort'nate ould cripple,' says he,
' and it's *I* that'll make you the sportin' bird.'

" With that, my dear, he took up the goose by the two
wings—' criss o' my crass on you,' says he, markin' her to
grace with the blessed sign at the same minute—and
throwin' her up in the air, ' whew !' says he, jist givin' her
a blast to help her; and with that, my jewel, she tuk to
her heels, flyin' like one of the aigles themselves, and
cuttin' as many capers as a swallow before a shower of
rain. Away she wint down there, right forninst you, along
the side of the clift, and flew over Saint Kavin's bed (that
is where Saint Kavin's bed is *now* but was not *thin*, by
raison it wasn't made, but was conthrived afther by Saint

Kavin himself, that the women might lave him alone), and on with her undher Luduff, and round the ind av the lake there, far beyunt where you see the watherfall (though indeed it's no watherfall at all now, but only a poor dhribble av a thing; but if you seen it in the winther, it id do your heart good, and it roarin' like mad, and as white as the dhriven snow, and rowlin' down the big rocks before, all as one as childher playin' marbles)—and on with her thin right over the lead mines o' Luganure (that is where the lead mines is *now*, but was not *thin*, by raison they worn't discovered, *but was all goold in Saint Kavin's time*). Well, over the ind o' Luganure she flew, stout and sturdy, and round the other ind av the *little* lake, by the Churches (that is, *av coorse*, where the Churches is *now*, but was not *thin*, by raison they wor not built, but aftherwards by Saint Kavin), and over the big hill here over your head, where you see the big clift (and that clift in the mountain was made by *Fan Ma Cool*, where he cut it acrass with a big swoord, that he got made a purpose by a blacksmith out o' Rathdrum, a cousin av his own, for to fight a joyant [giant] that darr'd him an the Curagh o' Kildare; and he thried the swoord first an the mountain, and cut it down into a gap, as is plain to this day; and faith, sure enough, it's the same sauce he sarv'd the joyant, soon and suddent, and chopped him in two like a pratie, for the glory of his sowl and ould Ireland)—well, down she flew over the clift, and flutterin' over the wood there at Poulanass (where I showed you the purty waterfall—and by the same token, last Thursday was a twelvemonth sence a young lady, Miss Rafferty by name, fell into the same watherfall, and was nigh hand drownded—and indeed would be to this day, but for a young man that jumped in afther her; indeed a smart slip iv a young man he was—he was out o' Francis Street, I hear, and coorted her sence, and they wor married, I'm given to undherstand—and indeed a purty couple they wor.) Well—as I said—afther flutterin' over the wood a little bit, to *plaze* herself, the goose flew down, and lit at the foot o' the king, as fresh as a daisy, afther flyin' roun' his dominions, just as if she hadn't flew three perch.

" Well, my dear, it was a beautiful sight to see the king standin' with his mouth open, lookin' at his poor ould goose flyin' as light as a lark, and betther nor ever she was ; and when she lit at his fut, he patted her an the head, and ' *Ma vourneen*,' says he, ' but you are the *darlint* o' the world.'

" ' And what do you say to me,' says Saint Kavin, ' for makin' her the like ?'

' " By gor,' says the King, ' I say nothin' bates the art o' man, barrin' the bees.'

" ' And do you say no more nor that ?' says Saint Kavin.

" ' And that I'm behoulden to you,' says the king.

" ' But will you gi' me all the ground the goose flewn over,' says Saint Kavin.

" ' I will,' says King O'Toole, ' and you're welkim to it,' says he, ' though its the last acre I have to give.'

" ' But you'll keep your word thrue ?' says the saint.

" ' As thrue as the sun,' says the king.

" ' It's well for you,' (says Saint Kavin, mighty sharp)— ' it's well for you, King O'Toole, that you said that word,' says he ; ' for if you didn't say that word, *the divil receave the bit o' your goose id ever fly agin*,' says Saint Kavin.

" Oh, you needn't laugh," said old Joe, half offended at detecting the trace of a suppressed smile ; " you needn't laugh, *for it's thruth I'm tellin' you.*

" Well, when the king was as good as his word, Saint Kavin was *plazed* with him, and then it was that he made himself known to the king. ' And,' says he, ' King O'Toole, you're a decent man,' says he, ' for I only kem here to *thry you.* You don't know me,' says he, ' bekase I'm disguised.'

" ' Troth, then, you're right enough,' says the king. ' I

didn't perceave it,' says he; 'for indeed I never seen the sign o' sper'ts an you.'

"'Oh! that's not what I mane,' says Saint Kavin; 'I mane I'm deceavin' you all out, and that I'm not myself at all.'

"'Blur-an-agers, thin,' says the king, 'if you're not yourself, who are you?'

"'I'm Saint Kavin,' said the saint, blessin' himself.

"'Oh, queen iv heaven!' says the king, makin' the sign o' the crass betune his eyes, and fallin' down on his knees before the saint. 'Is it the great Saint Kavin,' says he, 'that I've been discoorsin' all this time without knowin' it,' says he, 'all as one as if he was a lump iv a *gossoon?* —and so you're a saint!' says the king.

"'I am,' says Saint Kavin.

"'By gor, I thought I was only talking to a dacent boy,' says the king.

"'Well, you know the differ now,' says the saint. 'I'm Saint Kavin,' says he, 'the greatest of all the saints.'

"For Saint Kavin, you must know, sir," added Joe, treating me to another parenthesis, "Saint Kavin is counted the greatest of all the saints, because he went to school with the prophet Jeremiah.

"Well, my dear, that's the way that the place kem, all at wanst, into the hands of Saint Kavin; for the goose flewn round every individyial acre of King O'Toole's property you see, *bein' let into the saycret* by Saint Kavin, who was mighty *cute;* and so, when he *done* the ould king out of his property for the glory of God, he was *plazed* with him, and he and the king was the best o' friends iver more afther (for the poor ould king was *doatin'*, you see), and the king had his goose as good as new, to divart him as long as he lived; and the saint supported him afther he kem into his property, as I tould you, antil the day iv his death—and that was soon afther; for the poor goose thought he was ketchin' a throut one Friday; but, my

jewel, it was a mistake he made, and instead of a throut
it was a thievin' horse-eel. By dad, the eel killed the
king's goose—and small blame to him; but he didn't ate
her, bekase he daren't ate what Saint Kavin laid his
blessed hands on.

"Howsumdever, the king never recovered the loss iv
his goose, though he had her stuffed (I don't mane stuffed
with praties and inyans, but as a curiosity), and presarved
in a glass case for his own divarshin; and the poor king
died on the next Michaelmas Day, which was remarkable.
Troth, it's thruth I'm tellin' you. And when he was gone,
St. Kavin gev him an illigant wake and a beautiful berry-
in'; and more betoken, he *said mass for his sowl, and tuk
care av his goose.*"

FATHER ROACH.

SAMUEL LOVER.

This story is founded on fact, and exhibits a trial of patience that one
wonders human nature could support. Passive endurance, we know, is
more difficult than active, and that which is recorded in the following tale
is strictly true.

Father Roach was a good Irish priest,
Who stood, in his stocking-feet, six feet, at least.
I don't mean to say he'd six feet in his stockings;
He only had two—so leave off with your mockings—
I know that you think I was making a blunder:
If Paddy says lightning, you think he means thunder:
So I'll say, in his boots Father Roach stood to view
A fine, comely man of six feet two.

Oh, a pattern was he of a true Irish priest,
To carve the big goose at the big wedding feast,
To peel the big *pratie*, and take the big can
(With a very big picture upon it of "Dan").
To pour out the punch for the bridegroom and bride,
Who sat smiling and blushing on either side,
While their health went around, and the innocent glee
Rang merrily under the old roof-tree.

Father Roach had a very big parish,
By the very big name of Knockdundherumdharish,
With plenty of bog, and with plenty of mountain:
The miles he'd to travel would throuble you countin'.
The duties were heavy to go through them all—
Of the wedding and christ'ning, the mass and sick-call—
Up early, down late, was the good parish pastor:
Few ponies than his were obliged to go faster.

He'd a big pair of boots and a purty big pony,
The boots greased with fat—but the baste was but bony;
For the pride of the flesh was so far from the pastor,
That the baste thought it manners to copy his master:
And, in this imitation, the baste, by degrees,
Would sometimes attempt to go down on his knees;
But in this too-great freedom the Father soon stopped him,
With a dig of the spurs—or, if need be, he whopp'd him.

And Father Roach had a very big stick,
Which could make very thin any crowd he found thick:
In a fair he would rush through the heat of the action,
And scatter, like chaff to the wind, every faction;
If the *leaders* escaped from the strong holy man,
He made sure to be down on the *heads* of the clan;
And the Blackfoot who courted each foeman's approach,
Faith, 'tis hot-foot he'd fly from the stout Father Roach.

Father Roach had a very big mouth,
For the brave, broad brogue of the beautiful South;
In saying the mass sure his fine voice was famous,
It would do your heart good just to hear his " OREMUS,"
Which brought down the broad-shouldered boys to their knees,
As *aisy* as winter shakes leaves from the trees;
But the rude blast of winter could never approach
The power of the sweet voice of good Father Roach.

Father Roach had a very big heart,
And " a way of his own"—far surpassing all art;
His joke sometimes carried reproof to a clown;
He could chide with a smile—as the thistle sheds down.
He was simple, tho' sage—he was gentle, yet strong;
When he gave good advice he ne'er made it too long,

But just rolled it up like a snowball, and pelted
It into your ear—where, in softness, it melted.

The good Father's heart, in its unworldly blindness,
Overflowed with the milk of human kindness;
And he gave it so freely, the wonder was great
That it lasted so long—for, come early or late,
The unfortunate had it. Now some people deem
This milk is so precious, they keep it for cream;
But that's a mistake—for it spoils by degrees,
And, tho' exquisite milk, it makes very bad cheese.

You'll pause to inquire, and with wonder, perchance,
How so many perfections are placed, at a glance,
In your view, of a poor Irish priest, who was fed
On potatoes, perhaps, or at most griddle bread;
Who ne'er rode in a coach, and whose simple abode
Was a homely thatch'd cot on a wild mountain road;
To whom dreams of a mitre never occurred;—
I will tell you the cause, then—and just in *one word*.

Father Roach had a MOTHER, who shed
Round the innocent days of his infant bed
The influence holy, which early inclin'd
In heavenward direction the boy's gentle mind,
And stamp'd there the lessons its softness could take,
Which, strengthened in manhood, no power could shake:
In vain might the Demon of Darkness approach
The mother-made virtue of good Father Roach!

Father Roach had a brother beside;
His mother's own darling—his brother's fond pride;
Great things were expected from Frank, when the world
Should see his broad banner of talent unfurl'd.
But Fate cut him short—for the murderer's knife
Abridg'd the young days of Frank's innocent life;
And the mass for *his* soul was the only approach
To comfort now left for the fond Father Roach.

Father Roach had a penitent grim
Coming, of late, to confession to him;

He was rank in vice—he was steeped in crime.
The reverend Father, in all his time,
So dark a confession had never known
As that now made to th' Eternal Throne;
And when he ask'd was the catalogue o'er,
The sinner replied—" I've a thrifle more."

" A trifle ?—what mean you, dark sinner, say ?
A trifle ?—Oh, think of your dying day !
A trifle *more?*—what more dare meet
The terrible eye of the Judgment-seat
Than all I have heard ?—The oath broken—the theft
Of a poor maiden's honor—'twas all she had left !
Say what have you done that worse could be ?"
He whispered, " Your brother was murdered by me."

' O God !" groan'd the Priest, " but the trial is deep,
My own brother's murder a secret to keep,
And minister here to the murderer of mine—
But not *my* will, O FATHER, but *thine !*"
Then the penitent said, " You will not betray ?"
" What, I ?—thy confessor ? Away, away !"
" Of penance, good Father, what cup shall I drink ?"
Drink the dregs of thy life—live on, and *think !*"

The hypocrite penitent cunningly found
This means of suppressing suspicion around.
Would the murderer of Frank e'er confess to his brother ?
He, surely, was guiltless—it must be some other.
And years roll'd on, and the only record
'Twixt the murderer's hand and the eye of THE LORD
Was that brother—by rule of his Church decreed
To silent knowledge of guilty deed.

Twenty or more of years passed away,
And locks once raven were growing gray,
And some, whom the Father once christen'd, now stood,
In the ripen'd bloom of womanhood,
And held at the font *their* babies' brow
For the holy sign and the sponsor's vow;
And grandmothers smil'd by their wedded girls ;
But the eyes once diamonds, the teeth once pearls,

The casket of beauty no longer grace;
Mem'ry, fond mem'ry alone, might trace
Through the mist of years a dreamy light
Gleaming afar from the gems once bright.

Oh, Time! how varied is thy sway
'Twixt beauty's growth and dim decay!
By fine degrees, beneath thy hand,
Does latent loveliness expand;

The coral casket richer grows
With its second pearly dow'r;
The brilliant eye still brighter glows
With the maiden's ripening hour:—
So gifted are ye of Time, fair girls;
But Time, while his gift he deals,
From the sunken socket the diamond steals,
And takes back to his waves the pearls!

*   *   *   *   *   *

It was just at this time that a man, rather sallow,
Whose cold eye burn'd dim in his features of tallow,
Was seen, at a cross-way, to mark the approach
Of the kind-hearted parish-priest, good Father Roach.
A deep salutation he render'd the Father,
Who return'd it but coldly, and seem'd as he'd rather
Avoid the same track;—so he struck o'er a hill,
But the sallow intruder *would* follow him still.

" Father," said he, " as I'm going your way,
A word on the road to your Reverence I'd say.
Of late so entirely I've altered my plan,
Indeed, holy sir, I'm a different man;
I'm thinking of wedding, and bettering my lot—"
The Father replied, " You had better not."
" Indeed, reverend sir, my wild oats are all sown."
" But perhaps," said the Priest, " they are not yet *grown* :—

" At least they're not *reap'd*,"—and his look became keener;
" And ask not a woman to be your gleaner—
You have my advice!"   The Priest strode on,
And silence ensued, as one by one

They pass'd through a deep defile, which wound
Through the lonely hills—and the solemn profound
Of the silence was broken alone by the cranch
Of their hurried tread on some wither'd branch.

The sallow man followed the Priest so fast,
That the setting sun their one shadow cast.
" Why press," said the Priest, "so close to me ?"
The follower answered convulsively,
 As, gasping and pale, through the hollow he hurried,
" 'Tis here, close by, poor Frank is buried—"
" *What* Frank?" said the Priest—"*What* Frank?" cried the
          other;
" Why, he whom I slew—your brother—your brother."

" Great God !" cried the Priest—" in thine own good time,
Thou liftest the veil from the hidden crime.
Within the confessional, dastard, the seal
Was set on my lips, which might never reveal
What *there* was spoken; but now the sun,
The daylight hears what thine arm hath done,
And now, under heaven, my arm shall bring
Thy felon neck to the hempen string !"

Pale was the murd'rer, and paler the Priest—
O Destiny !—rich was indeed thy feast
In that awful hour !—The victim stood
His own accuser;—the Pastor good,
Freed from the chain of silence, spoke ;
No more the confessional's terrible yoke
Made him run, neck and neck, with a murderer in peace,
And the villain's life had run out its lease.

The jail, the trial, conviction came,
And honor was given to the poor Priest's name,
Who held, for years, the secret dread
Of a murderer living—a brother dead,
And still, by the rule of his Church compell'd,
The awful mystery in silence held,
Till the murderer himself did the secret broach—
A triumph to justice and Father Roach.

PETER MULROONEY AND THE BLACK FILLY.

An Irish Recitation.

Kitchen maids are so often bothered in their household duties by the gallantries of the men servants, that my wife had selected one from the Congo race of negroes, ugly to look at, but good-tempered, and black as your hat. Phillis was her name, and a more faithful, devoted, and patient creature we never had around us. I have thus introduced her to my hearers, because she was a conspicuous personage in some of the droll incidents connected with my taking into service a queer specimen of a Patlander, by name Peter Mulrooney.

Mulrooney applied to me for a situation as groom, in the place of one I had just dismissed; and on my inquiring if he could give me a reference as to his character and qualifications, he mentioned the name of Mr. David Urban (a personal friend of mine), with whom he had lived. "An sure," said he with enthusiasm, "there isn't a dacenter jintleman in all Ameriky."

"I am happy to hear him so well spoken of," said I, "but if you were so much attached to him, why did you quit his service?"

"Sorra one o' me knows," said he, a little evasively, as I thought. "Ayeh! but 'twasn't his fault, anyhow."

"I dare say not; but what did you do after you left Mr. Urban?"

"Och, bad luck to me, sir! 'twas the foolishest thing in the world. I married a widdy, sir."

"And became a householder, eh?"

"Augh!" he exclaimed, with an expression of intense disgust, "the house wouldn't hould me long; 'twas too hot for that, I does be thinkin'."

"Humph! You found the widow too fond of having her own way, I suppose?"

"Thrue for you, sir; an' a mighty crooked way it was, that same, an' that's no lie."

"She managed to keep you straight, I dare say."

"Straight! Och, by the powhers, Misther Stanley, ye may say that! If I'd swallowed a soger's ramrod, 'tisn't straighter I'd have been!"

"And the result was, that, not approving the widow's discipline, you ran away and left her?"

"Sure sir, 'twas asier done nor that. Her first husband, betther luck to him, saved me the throuble."

"Her first husband! had she another husband living?"

"Oh, yis, sir; one Mike Connolly, a sayfarin' man who was reported dead; but he came back one day, an' I resthored him his wife and childher. Oh, but 'twas a proud man I was, to be able to comfort poor Mike, by givin' him his lost wife—an' he so grateful, too! Ah, sir, he had a ra'al Irish heart."

Being favorably impressed with Peter's genuine good humor, I concluded to take him at once into my service. Nor was I mistaken in his character, for he took excellent care of my horses, and kept everything snug around the stables. One day I thought I would test his usefulness in doctoring, so I sent for him to the house.

"Peter," said I, "do you think I could trust you to give the black filly a warm mash this evening?"

As he stared at me for a minute or two without replying, I repeated the question.

"Is it a mash, sir?" said he. "Sure, an' I'd like to be plasin' yer honor any way, an' that's no lie."

As he spoke, however, I fancied I saw a strange sort of puzzled expression flit across his face.

"I beg pardin, sir," continued he, "but 'tis bothered I am; will I be afther givin' her an ould counthry mash, or an Ameriky mash?"

"I don't know if there is any difference between them," I answered, rather puzzled at what he was aiming, but

I found afterwards that he didn't know what a mash was.

"Arrah, 'tis rasonable enough ye shouldn't," said Peter, "considerin' that yer honor niver set fut in ould Ireland."

"Look here, Mulrooney," said I, impatiently, "I want you to put about two double handfuls of bran into a pail of warm water, and, after stirring the mixture well, give it to the black filly. That is what we call a bran mash in this country. Now, do you perfectly understand me?"

"Good luck to yer honor!" replied Peter, looking much relieved; for he had got the information he was fishing for. "Good luck to yer honor! what 'ud I be good for, if I didn't? sure, 'tis the ould counthry mash afther all."

"Perhaps so, but be sure you make no mistake."

"Oh, niver fear, sir, I'll do it illegant; but about the warm wather?"

"There's plenty to be had in the kitchen."

"An' the naygur? Will I say till her it's yer honor's orthers?" inquired Peter, earnestly.

"Certainly; she'll make no difficulty."

"Oh, begorra! 'tisn't a traneen I care for that; but will I give her the full ov the bucket, sir?"

"'Twill do her no harm," said I, carelessly. With that Peter made his best bow and left my presence.

It might have been some fifteen minutes after this that my wife, who was a little unwell that day, came into the sitting-room, saying, "I wish you'd go into the kitchen, George, and see what's the difficulty between that Irishman and Phillis; I am afraid they are quarreling."

At that moment we heard a crash and a suppressed shriek. I hurried from the room, and soon heard, as I passed through the hall, an increasing clamor in the kitchen beyond. First came the shrill voice of Phillis.

"You jess lebe me 'lone, now, will yer? I won't hab nuffin to do wid de stuff, nairaway."

"You ugly an' conthrary ould nayger, don't I tell ye 'tis the masther's ordhers?" I heard Peter respond.

"Tain't no sech ting. Go way, you poor white Irish trash! who ebber heard ob 'spectable color'd woman a takin' a bran mash, I'd like to know."

The reality of Peter's ridiculous blunder flashed upon me at once, and the fun of the thing struck me so irresistibly, that I hesitated for a moment to break in upon it.

"Arrah, be aisy, can't ye? an' be afther takin' it down like a dacent naygur," I heard Peter say.

"Go way, you feller," screamed Phillis, "or I'll call missis, dat I will."

"Och, be this an' be that!" says Peter, resolutely, "if 'tis about to frighten the beautiful misthress ye are, and she sick, too, at this same time, I'll be afther puttin' a shtop to that."

Immediately afterwards came a short scuffle, and then a stifled scream. Concluding that it was now time for me to interfere, I moved quickly on, and just as the scuffling gave way to smothered sobs and broken ejaculations, I flung open the door and looked in. The first thing that caught my eye was Phillis seated in a chair, sputtering and gasping; while Mulrooney, holding her head under his left arm, was employing his right hand in conveying a tin cup of bran mash from the bucket at his side to her upturned mouth.

"What in the name of all that is good are you doing now, Peter?" said I.

"Sure, sir, what wud I do but give black Phillis the warm mash, accordin' to yer honor's ordhers? Augh! the haythen. Bad cess to her! 'tis throuble enough I've had to make her rasonable and obadient, an' that's no lie—the stupid ould thafe of a nagur."

The reader may imagine the finale to so rich a scene; even my wife, sick as she was, caught the infection, and laughed heartily. As for Peter, the last I heard of him that evening was his muttering, as he walked away—

"Ayeh! why didn't he tell me? If they call naygurs fillies, and horses fillies, sure an' how the divil should I know the differ?"

Peter remained in my service five years, during which period he treated Phillis with great deference.

PHAIDRIG CROHOORE.

A Favorite Irish Recitation.

Oh! Phaidrig Crohoore was the broth of a boy, and he stood six
    feet eight;
And his arm was as round as another man's thigh—'tis Phaidrig
    was great;
And his hair was as black as the shadows of night,
And hung over the scars left by many a fight;

And his voice, like the thunder, was deep, strong and loud,
And his eye like the lightnin' from under the cloud.
And all the girls liked him, for he could speak civil
And sweet when he chose it, for he was the divil.

An' there wasn't a girl, from thirty-five under,
Divil a matter how cross, but he could come round her.
But of all the sweet girls that smiled on him, but one
Was the girl of his heart, an' he loved her alone.

An' warm as the sun, as the rock firm and sure
Was the love of the heart of Phaidrig Crohoore;
An' he'd die for one smile from his Kathleen O'Brien,
For his love, like his hatred, was sthrong as a lion.

But Michael O'Hanlon loved Kathleen as well
As he hated Crohoore, an' that same was like hell.
But O'Brien liked him, for they were the same parties,
The O'Briens, O'Hanlons, an' Murphys, and Carthys—

An' they all went together an' hated Crohoore,
For it's many's the batin' he gave them before:

An' O'Hanlon made up to O'Brien, an' says he—
" I'll marry your daughter if you'll give her to me."

An' the match was made up, an' Shrovetide came on,
The company assimbled, three hundred if one—
There was all the O'Hanlons and Murphys and Carthys
An' the young boys an' girls av all o' them parties.

An' the O'Briens, av coorse, gathered sthrong on that day,
An' the pipers and fiddlers were tearin' away ;
There was roarin', an' jumpin', an' jiggin,' an' flingin',
An' jokin', an' blessin', an' kissin', an' singin'.

An' they all were a-laughin'—why not, to be sure ?
How O'Hanlon came inside of Phaidrig Crohoore !
An' they all talked and laughed the length of the table,
Aitin' an' drinkin' all while they were able ;

An' with pipin', an' fiddlin', an' roarin' like thunder,
Your head you'd think fairly was splittin asunder.
And the priest call'd out—" Silence, ye blackguards, agin !"
An' he tuk up his prayer-book, just goin' to begin.

And they all held their tongue from their funnin' and bawlin' ;
So silent you'd notice the smallest pin fallin' ;
And the priest just beginnin' to read—when the door
Sprung back to the wall, and in walked Crohoore.

Oh ! Phaidrig Crohoore was the broth of a boy, an' he stood six
    feet eight,
An' his arm was as round as another man's thigh—'tis Phaidrig
    was great !
An' he walked slowly up, watched by many a bright eye,
As a black cloud moves on through the stars of the sky.

An' none strove to stop him, for Phaidrig was great,
Till he stood all alone, just opposite the sate
Where O'Hanlon and Kathleen, his beautiful bride,
Were sittin' so illigant out side by side.

An' he gave her one look that her heart almost broke,
An' he turned to O'Brien, her father, and spoke ;
An' his voice, like the thunder, was deep, sthrong an' loud,
An' his eyes shone like lightniu' from under the cloud :

"I didn't come here like a tame crawlin' mouse,
But I stand like a man in my inimy's house;
In the field, on the road, Phaidrig never knew fear
Of his foeman, an' God knows he scorns it here.

So lave me at aise for three minutes or four
To spake to the girl I'll never see more."
An' to Kathleen he turned, and his voice changed its tone,
For he thought of the days when he called her his own.

An' his eyes blazed like lightnin' from under the cloud
On his false-hearted girl, reproachful and proud.
An' says he, " Kathleen bawn, is it thrue what I hear,
That you marry of your own free choice, without threat or fear ?

If so, spake the word, and I'll turn and depart,
Chated once, and once only, by woman's false heart."
Oh! sorrow and love made the poor girl dumb,
An' she tried hard to spake, but the words wouldn't come;

For the sound of his voice, as he stood there fornint her,
Wint could on her heart as the night wind in winther;
An' the tears in her blue eyes stood tremblin' to flow,
An' pale was her cheek as the moonshine on snow.

Then the heart of bould Phaidrig swelled high in its place,
For he knew, by one look in that beautiful face,
That the strangers an' foemen their pledged hands might sever,
Her true heart was his, and his only, forever!

An' he lifted his voice, like the eagle's hoarse call,
An' says Phaidrig, " She's mine still, in spite of ye all !"
Then up jumped O'Hanlon, an' a tall boy was he,
An' he looked on bould Phaidrig as fierce as could be;

An' says he, " By the hokey, before ye go out,
Bould Phaidrig Crohoore, you must fight for a bout."
Then Phaidrig made answer, " I'll do my endeavor;"
An' with one blow he stretched bould Hanlon forever.

In his arms he took Kathleen an' stepped to the door,
An' he leaped on his horse, and flung her before ;
An' they all were so bothered that not a man stirred,
Till the gallopin' hoofs on the pavement was heard.

Then up they all started, like bees in the swarm,
An' they riz a great shout, like the burst of a storm,
An' they roared, an' they ran, an' they shouted galore;
But Kathleen and Phaidrig they never saw more.

But them days are gone by, an' he is now no more,
An' the green grass is growin' o'er Phaidrig Crohoore;
For he couldn't be aisy or quiet at all;
As he lived a brave boy, he resolved so to fall.

An' he took a good pike—for Phaidrig was great—
An' he fought and he died in the year ninety-eight.
An' the day that Crohoore in the green field was killed,
A sthrong boy was stretched, an' a sthrong heart was stilled.

DERMOT O'DOWD.

SAMUEL LOVER.

When Dermot O'Dowd coorted Molly McCann,
   They were as sweet as the honey and as soft as the down,
But when they were wed they began to find out
   That Dermot could storm, and that Molly could frown;
They would neither give in—so the neighbors gave out—
   Both were hot, till a coldness came over the two,
And Molly would flusther, and Dermot would blusther—
   Stamp holes in the flure, and cry out " *Weirasthru!*
      Oh, murther! I'm married!
      I wish I had tarried;
      I'm sleepless and speechless—no word can I say;
      My bed is no use—
      I'll give back to the goose
      The feathers I pluck'd on last Michaelmas Day."

" Ah," says Molly, " you once used to call me a bird."
" Faix, you're ready enough still to fly out," says he.
" You said then my eyes were as bright as the skies,
   And my lips like the rose—now no longer like me."
Says Dermot, " Your eyes are as bright as the morn,
   But your frown is as black as a big thunder cloud;
If your lip is a rose, faith your tongue is a thorn
   That sticks in the heart of poor Dermot O'Dowd."
Says Molly, " You once said my voice was a thrush,

But now it's a rusty old hinge with a creak."
Says Dermot, " You called me a duck when I coorted,
  But now I'm a goose every day in the week;
But all husbands are geese, though our pride it may shock,
  From the first 'twas ordained so by Nature, I fear;
Ould Adam himself was the first of the flock,
  And Eve, with her apple sauce, cook'd him, my dear."

PAT'S CRITICISM.

CHARLES F. ADAMS.

There's a story that's old,
  But good if twice told,
Of a doctor of limited skill,
  Who cured beast and man
  On the "cold water plan,"
Without the small help of a pill.
    On his portal of pine
    Hung an elegant sign
Depicting a beautiful rill,
    And a lake, where a sprite,
    With apparent delight,
Was sporting in sweet dishabille.
    Pat McCarty one day,
    As he sauntered that way,
Stood and gazed at that portal of pine,
    When the doctor with pride
    Stepped up to his side,
Saying: " Pat, how is that for a sign?"
    " There's wan thing," says Pat,
    " Ye've lift out o' that,
Which, be jabers, is quoite a mistake;
    It's trim and it's nate,
    But to make it complate,
Ye shud have a foine burd on the lake."
    " Ah! Indeed! pray then tell,
    To make it look well,
What bird do you think it may lack?'
    Says Pat, " Of the same
    I've forgotten the name,
But the song that he sings is 'quack!' 'quack!' "

PAT AND THE FOX.

SAMUEL LOVER.

A Humorous Irish Recitation.

"Paddy," said the squire, "perhaps you would favor the gentlemen with that story you told me once about a fox?"

"Indeed and I will, plaze yer honor," said Paddy, "though I know full well the divil a one word iv it you b'lieve, nor the gintlemen won't either, though you're axin' me for it—but only want to laugh at me, and call me a big liar when my back's turned."

"Maybe we wouldn't wait for your back being turned, Paddy, to honor you with that title."

"Oh, indeed, I'm not sayin' that you wouldn't do it as soon foreninst my face, your honor, as you often did before, and will agin, plaze God, and welkim."

"Well, Paddy, say no more about that, but let's have the story."

"Sure I'm losing no time, only telling the gintlemen beforehand that it's what they'll be callin' it, a lie—and indeed it's ancommon, sure enough; but you see, gintlemen, you must remimber that the fox is the cunnin'est baste in the world, barrin' the wran——"

Here Paddy was questioned why he considered the wren as cunning a *baste* as the fox.

"Why, sir, bekase all the birds build their nest wid one hole to it only, excep'n the wran; but the wran builds two holes to the nest, and so that if any inimy comes to disturb it upon one door it can go out an the other. But the fox is cute to that degree that there's many mortial a fool to him—and, by dad, the fox could buy and sell many a Christian, as you'll soon see by and by, when I tell you what happened to a wood-ranger that I knew wanst, and a dacent man he was, and wouldn't say the thing in a lie.

"Well, you see, he came home one night mighty tired—

for he was out wid a party in the domain cock-shootin' that
day; and whin he got back to his lodge he threw a few
logs o' wood an the fire to make himself comfortable, and
he tuk whatever little matther he had for his supper—and
afther that he felt himself so tired that he wint to bed.
But you're to understand that, though he wint to bed, it
was more for to rest himself like, than to sleep, for it was
airly; and so he jist wint into bed, and there he divarted
himself lookin' at the fire, that was blazin' as merry as a
bonfire an the hearth.

" Well, as he was lyin' that-a-way, jist thinkin' o' nothin'
at all, what should come into the place but a fox. But I
must tell you, what I forgot to tell you before, that the
ranger's house was on the bordhers o' the wood, and he had
no one to live wid him but himself, barrin' the dogs that
he had the care iv, that was his only companions, and he
had a hole cut an the door, with a swingin' boord to it,
that the dogs might go in or out accordin' as it plazed thim;
and, by dad, the fox came in as I told you, through the
hole in the door, as bould as a ram, and walked over to the
fire, and sat down foreninst it.

" Now it was mighty provokin' that all the dogs was out;
they wor rovin' about the wood, you see, lookin' for to
catch rabbits to ate, or some other mischief, and so it happened that there wasn't as much as one individual dog in
the place; and, by gor, I'll go bail the fox knew that right
well before he put his nose inside the ranger's lodge.

" Well, the ranger was in hopes some o' the dogs id come
home and ketch the chap, and he was loath to stir hand or
fut himself, afeared o' frightenin' away the fox, but by gor,
he could hardly keep his timper at all at all, whin he seen
the fox take his pipe aff o' the hob where he left it afore he
wint to bed, and puttin' the bowl o' the pipe into the fire
to kindle it (it's as thrue as I'm here), he began to smoke
foreninst the fire, as nath'ral as any other man you ever seen.

" 'Musha, bad luck to your impidence, you long-tailed

blackguard,' says the ranger, 'and is it smokin' my pipe you are? Oh, thin, by this and by that, iv I had my gun convaynient to me, it's fire and smoke of another sort, and what you wouldn't bargain for, I'd give you,' says he. But still he was loath to stir, hopin' the dogs id come home; and 'By gor, my fine fellow,' says he to the fox, 'if one o' the dogs comes home, saltpethre wouldn't save you, and that's a sthrong pickle.'

"So with that he watched antil the fox wasn't mindin' him, but was busy shakin' the cindhers out o' the pipe whin he was done wid it, and so the ranger thought he was goin' to go immediately afther gettin' an air o' the fire and a shough o' the pipe; and so, says he, ' Faix, my lad, I won't let you go so aisy as all that, as cunnin' as you think yourself;' and with that he made a dart out o' bed, and run over to the door, and got betune it and the fox, 'And now,' says he, ' your bread's baked, my buck, and maybe my lord won't have a fine run out o' you, and the dogs at your brish every yard, you morodin' thief, and the divil mind you,' says he, ' for your impidence—for sure, if you hadn't the impidence of a highwayman's horse it's not into my very house, undher my nose, you'd daar for to come:' and with that he began to whistle for the dogs; and the fox, that stood oyein' him all the time while he was spakin', began to think it was time to be joggin' whin he heard the whistle—and says the fox to himself, ' Troth, indeed, you think yourself a mighty great ranger now,' says he, ' and you think you're very cute, but upon my tail, and that's a big oath, I'd be long sorry to let such a mallet-headed bog-throtter as yourself take a dirty advantage o' me, and I'll engage,' says the fox, ' I'll make you lave the door soon and suddint,'—and with that he turned to where the ranger's brogues was lyin' hard by beside the fire, and, what would you think, but the fox tuk up one o' the brogues, and wint over to the fire, and threw it into it.

" ' I think that'll make you start,' says the fox.

" 'Divil resave the start,' says the ranger—' that won't do, my buck,' says he, ' the brogue may burn to cindhers,' says he, ' but out o' this I won't stir; ' and thin, puttin' his fingers into his mouth, he gev a blast iv a whistle you'd hear a mile off, and shouted for the dogs.

" ' So that won't do,' says the fox—' well, I must thry another offer,' says he, and with that he tuk up the other brogue, and threw it into the fire too.

" ' There, now,' says he, ' you may keep the other company,' says he; ' and there's a pair o' you now, as the divil said to his knee-buckles.'

" ' Oh, you thievin' varment,' says the ranger, ' you won't lave me a tack to my feet ; but no matter,' says he, ' your head's worth more nor a pair o' brogues to me any day, and by the Piper of Blessintown, you're money in my pocket this minit,' says he : and with that, the fingers was in his mouth agin, and he was goin' to whistle, whin, what would you think, but up sets the fox an his hunkers, and puts his two forepaws into his mouth, makin' game o' the ranger—(bad luck to the lie I tell you.)

" Well, the ranger, and no wondher, although in a rage as he was, couldn't help laughin' at the thought o' the fox mockin' him, and, by dad, he tuk sitch a fit o' laughin' that he couldn't whistle—and that was the cuteness o' the fox to gain time ; but whin his first laugh was over, the ranger recovered himself, and gev another whistle; and so says the fox, ' By my sowl,' says he, ' I think it wouldn't be good for my health to stay here much longer, and I mustn't be triflin' with that blackguard ranger any more,' says he, ' and I must make him sensible that it is time to let me go, and though he hasn't understandin' to be sorry for his brogues, I'll go bail I'll make him lave that,' says he, ' before he'd say *sparables*'—and with that what do you think the fox done ? By all that's good—and the ranger himself told me out iv his own mouth, and said he would never have b'lieved it, ownly he seen it—the fox tuk a lighted piece iv a log out o' the blazin' fire, and run over wid it to the ranger's bed, and was goin' to throw it into the sthraw, and burn him out of house and home; so when the ranger seen that he gev a shout out iv him—

"'Hillo! hillo! you murtherin' villain,' says he, 'you're worse nor Captain Rock; is it goin' to burn me out you are, you red rogue iv a Ribbonman?' and he made a dart betune him and the bed, to save the house from bein' burnt,—but, my jew'l, that was all the fox wanted—and as soon as the ranger quitted the hole in the door that he was standin' foreninst, the fox let go the blazin' faggit, and made one jump through the door and escaped.

"But before he wint, the ranger gev me his oath that the fox turned round and gev him the most contemptible look he ever got in his life, and showed every tooth in his head with laughin', and at last he put out his tongue at him, as much as to say—'You've missed me like your mammy's blessin',' and off wid him, like a flash o' lightnin'.'"

MICKEY FREE AND THE PRIEST.

A Laughable Irish Recitation. CHARLES LEVER.

Mickey Free was a devout Catholic, in the same sense that he was enthusiastic about anything, that is, he believed and obeyed exactly as far as suited his own peculiar notions of comfort and happiness; beyond *that* his skepticism stepped in and saved him from inconvenience, and though he might have been somewhat puzzled to reduce his faith to a rubric, still it answered his purpose, and that was all he wanted. * * * * *

"Ah, then, Misther Charles," said he, with a half-suppressed yawn at the long period of probation his tongue had been undergoing in silence, "ah, then, but ye were mighty near it."

"Near what?" said I.

"Faith, then, myself doesn't well know; some say it's purgathory; but it's hard to tell."

"I thought you were too good a Catholic, Mickey, to show any doubts on the matter?"

"Maybe I am—maybe I ain't," was the cautious reply.

"Wouldn't Father Roach explain any of your difficulties for you, if you went over to him?"

"Faix it's little I'd mind his explaiuings."

"And why not?"

"Easy enough. If you ax ould Miles there without, what does he be doing with all the powther and shot, wouldn't he tell you he's shooting the rooks, and the magpies, and some other varmint? but myself knows he sells it to Widow Casey at two and fourpence a pound; so belikes Father Roach may be shooting away at the poor souls in purgathory, that all this time are enjoying the hoith of foin living in heaven, ye understand."

"And you think that's the way of it, Mickey?"

"Troth, it's likely. Anyhow, I know it's not the place they make it out."

"Why, how do you mean?"

"Well, then, I'll tell you, Misther Charles; but you must not be saying anything about it afther, for I don't like to talk about these kind of things."

Having pledged myself to the requisite silence and secrecy, Mickey began:

"Maybe you heard tell of the way my father—rest his soul wherever he is—came to his end. Well, I needn't mind particulars, but, in short, he was murdered in Ballinasloe one night, when he was batin' the whole town with a blackthorn stick he had, more betoken, a piece of a scythe was stack at the end of it; a nate weapon, and one he was mighty partial to; but these murdering thieves, the cattle dealers, that never cared for diversion of any kind, fell on him and broke his skull.

"Well, we had a very agreeable wake, and plenty of the best of everything, and to spare, and I thought it was all over; but somehow, though I paid father Roach fifteen shillings, and made him mighty drunk, he always gave me a black look wherever I met him, and when I took off my hat he'd turn away his head displeased like.

" 'Murder and ages,' said I, ' what's this for ?' but as I've a light heart I bore up, and didn't think more about it. One day, however, I was coming home from Athlone market, by myself on the road, when Father Roach overtook me. ' Devil a one o' me 'll take any notice of you now,' says I, ' and we'll see what 'll come out of it.' So the priest rid up, and looked me straight in the face.

" 'Mickey,' says he, ' Mickey.'

" 'Father,' says I.

" 'Is it that way you salute your clargy,' says he, ' with your caubeen on your head ?'

" 'Faix,' says I, ' it's little ye mind whether it's an or aff, for you never take the trouble to say by your leave, or divil take ye, or any other politeness, when we meet.'

" 'You're an ungrateful creature,' says he, ' and if you only knew, you'd be trembling in your skin before me this minute.'

" 'Devil a tremble,' says I, ' after walking six miles this way.'

" 'You're an obstinate, hard-hearted sinner,' says he, ' and it's no use in telling you.'

" 'Telling me what ?' says I, for I was getting curious to make out what he meant.

" 'Mickey,' says he, changing his voice, and putting his head down close to me, ' Mickey, I saw your father last night.'

" 'The saints be merciful to us,' said I, ' did ye ?'

" 'I did,' said he.

" 'Tear-an-ages,' says I, ' did he tell you what he did with the new corduroys he bought in the fair ?'

"'Oh, then, you are a could-hearted creature,' says he, 'and I'll not lose time with you.' With that he was going to ride away, when I took hold of the bridle.

"'Father, darling,' says I, 'God pardon me, but them breeches is goin' between me an' my night's rest; but tell me about my father.'

"'Oh, then, he's in a melancholy state.'

"'Whereabouts is he?' says I.

"'In purgathory,' says he; 'but he won't be there long.'

"'Well,' says I, 'that's a comfort anyhow.'

"'I am glad you think so,' says he; 'but there's more of the other opinion.'

"'What's *that?*' says I.

"'That hell's worse.'

"'Oh! meila-murther,' says I, 'is that it!'

"'Ay, that's it.'

"Well, I was so terrified and frightened I said nothing for some time, but trotted along beside the priest's horse.

"'Father,' says I, 'how long will it be before they send him where you know?'

"'It will not be long now,' says he, 'for they're tired entirely with him; they've no peace night nor day,' says he. 'Mickey, your father is a mighty hard man.'

"'True for you, Father Roach,' says I to myself. 'If he had only the ould stick with the scythe in it, I wish them joy of his company.'

"'Mickey,' says he, 'I see you're grieved, and I don't wonder; sure, it's a great disgrace to a decent family.'

"'Troth it is,' says I, 'but my father always liked low company. Could nothing be done for him now, Father Roach?' says I, looking up in the priest's face.

"'I'm greatly afraid, Mickey; he was a bad man, a very bad man.'

"'And ye think he'll go there?' says I.

"'Indeed, Mickey, I have my fears.'

"'Upon my conscience,' says I, 'I believe you're right; he was always a restless crayture.'

"'But it doesn't depind on him,' says the priest, crossly.

"'And then, who then?' says I.

"'Upon yourself, Mickey Free,' says he; 'God pardon you for it too.'

"'Upon me?' says I.

"'Troth no less,' says he; 'how many masses was said for your father's soul?—how many aves?—how many paters?—answer me.'

"'Devil a one of me knows!—maybe twenty.'

"'Twenty, twenty—no, nor one.'

"'And why not?' says I, 'what for wouldn't you be helping a poor crayture out of trouble, when it wouldn't cost you more nor a handful of prayers?'

"'Mickey, I see,' says he in a solemn tone, 'you're worse nor a haythen; but ye couldn't be other—ye never come to yer duties.'

"'Well, Father,' says I, looking very penitent, 'how many masses would get him out?'

"'Now you talk like a sensible man,' says he; 'now, Mickey, I've hopes for you—let me see'—here he went countin' up his fingers, and numberin' to himself for five minutes—'Mickey,' says he, 'I've a batch coming out on Tuesday week, and if you were to make great exertions perhaps your father could come with them; that is av they made no objections.'

"'And what for would they?' says I; 'he was always the hoith of company, and av singing's allowed in them parts—'

"'God forgive you, Mickey, but yer in a benighted state,' says he, sighing.

"'Well,' says I, 'how'll we get him out on Tuesday week? for that's bringing things to a focus.'

"'Two masses in the mornin', fastin',' says Father Roach, half loud, 'is two, and two in the afternoon is four, and two at vespers is six,' says he; 'six masses a day for nine days is close by sixty masses—say sixty,' says he, 'and they'll cost you—mind, Mickey, and don't be telling it again—for it's only to yourself I'd make them so cheap —a matter of three pounds.'

"'Three pounds,' says I, 'be-gorra ye might as well ax me to give you the rock of Cashel.'

"'I'm sorry for ye, Mickey,' says he, gatherin' up the reins to ride off, 'I'm sorry for you; and the day will come when the neglect of your poor father will be a sore stroke agin yourself.'

"'Wait a bit, your reverence,' says I, 'wait a bit; would forty shillings get him out?'

"'Av coorse it wouldn't,' says he.

"'Maybe,' says I, coaxing, 'maybe, av you say that his son was a poor boy that lived by his industhry, and the times was bad?'

"'Not the least use,' says he.

"'Arrah, but it's hard-hearted they are,' thinks I; 'well, see now, I'll give you the money—but I can't afford it all at on'st—but I'll pay you five shillings a week—will that do?'

"'I'll do my endayvors,' says Father Roach; 'and I'll speak to them to trate him peaceably in the meantime.'

"Long life to your reverence, and do. Well, here now, here's five hogs to begin with; and, musha, but I never thought I'd be spending my loose change that-a-way.'

"Father Roach put the six tinpinnies in the pocket of his black leather breeches, said something in Latin, bid me good-morning, and rode off.

"Well, to make my story short, I worked late and early to pay the five shillings a week, and I did do it for three weeks regular; then I brought four and fourpence—then it came down to one and tenpence—then ninepence—and, at last, I had nothing at all to bring.

"'Mickey Free,' says the priest, 'ye must stir yourself—

your father is mighty displeased at the way you've been doing of late ; and av ye kept yer word, he'd been near out by this time.'

" ' Troth,' says I, ' it's a very expensive place.'

" ' By coorse it is,' says he, ' sure all the quality of the land's there. But, Mickey, my man, with a little exertion your father's business is done. What are you jinglin' in your pocket there ? '

" ' It's ten shillings, your reverence, I have to buy seed potatoes.'

" ' Hand it here, my son. Isn't it better your father be enjoying himself in Paradise, than ye were to have all the potatoes in Ireland ?'

" ' And how do you know,' says I, ' he's so near out ?'

" ' How do I know—how do I know—is it ? didn't I see him ? '

" ' See him ! tear-an-ages, was you down there again ?' says I.

" ' I was,' says he, ' I was down there for three-quarters of an hour yesterday evening, getting out Luke Kennedy's mother—decent people the Kennedys—never spared expense.'

" ' And ye seen my father ?' says I.

" ' I did,' says he ; ' he had an ould flannel waistcoat on, and a pipe sticking out of the pocket av it.'

" ' That's him,' said I ; ' had he a hairy cap ?'

" ' I didn't mind the cap,' says he, ' but av coorse he wouldn't have it on his head in that place.'

" ' There's for you,' says I ; ' did he speak to you ?'

" ' He did,' says Father Roach ; ' he spoke very hard about the way he was treated down there, that they were always jibin' and jeerin' him about *drink*, and fightin', and the courses he led up here, and that it was a queer thing, for the matter of ten shillings, he was to be kept there so long.'

" ' Well,' says I, taking out the ten shillings and counting it with one hand, ' we must do our best, anyhow—and ye think this will get him out surely ?'

" 'I know it will,' says he; 'for when Luke's mother was leaving the place, yer father saw the door open; he made a rush at it, and be-gorra, before it was shut he got his head and one shoulder outside av it, so that ye see a trifle more 'ill do it.'

" 'Faix, and yer reverence,' says I, 'you've lightened my heart this morning,' and I put the money back again into my pocket.

" 'Why, what do you mean ?' says he, growing very red, for he was angry.

" 'Just this,' says I, 'that I've saved my money; for av it was my father you seen, and that he got his head and one shoulder outside the door, oh, then, by the powers,' says I, ' the devil a jail or jailer from hell to Connaught id hold him; so, Father Roach, I wish you the top of the morning,' and I went away laughing; and from that da to this I never heard more of purgathory; and ye see, Misther Charles, I think I was right."

BIDDY'S TROUBLES.

"It's thru for me, Katy, that I never seed the like of this people afore. It's a sorry time I've been having since coming to this house, twelve months agone this week Thursday. Yer know, honey, that my fourth coosin, Ann Macarthy, recommended me to Mrs. Whaler, and told the lady that I knew about genteel housework and the likes; while at the same time I had niver seed inter an American lady's kitchen. So she engaged me, and my heart was jist ready to burst wid grief for the story that Ann had told, for Mrs. Whaler was a swate-spoken lady, and never looked cross-like in her life; that I knew by her smooth, kind face. Well, jist the first thing she told me to do, after I dressed the children, was to dress the ducks for dinner. I stood looking at the lady for a couple of minutes, before I could make out any meaning at all to her words. Thin I went searching after clothes for the ducks; and such a time as I had, to be sure. High and low I went, till at last my mistress axed me for what I was looking; and I told her the clothes for the ducks, to be sure. Och, how she scramed and laughed, till my face was as rid as the sun wid shame, and she showed me in her kind swate way what her meaning was. Thin she told me how to air the beds; and it was a day for me, indade, when I could go up chamber alone and clare up the rooms. One day Mrs. Whaler said to me:

" ' Biddy, an' ye may give the baby an airin', if yees will.'

" What should I do—and it's thru what I am saying this blessed minute—but go up-stairs wid the child, and shake i⁺ and then howld it out of the winder. Such a scraming and kicking as the baby gave—but I hild on the harder. Everybody thin in the strate looked up at me; at last mistthress came up to see what for was so much noise.

" 'I am thrying to air the baby,' I said, ' but it kicks and scrames dridfully.'

" "There was company down below; and when Mrs. Whaler told them what I had been after doing, I thought they would scare the folks in the strate wid scraming.

" And then I was told I must do up Mr. Whaler's sharts one day when my mistress was out shopping. She told me repeatedly to do them up nice, for master was going away, so I takes the sharts and did them all up in some paper that I was after bringing from the ould country wid me, and tied some nice pink ribbon around the bundle.

" ' Where are the sharts, Biddy?' axed Mrs. Whaler, when she comed home.

" 'I have been doing them up in a quair nice way,' I said, bringing her the bundle.

" 'Will you iver be done wid your graneness ?' she axed me with a loud scrame.

"I can't for the life of me be tellin' what their talkin' manes. At home we call the likes of this fine work starching; and a deal of it I have done, too. Och! and may the blessed Vargin pity me, for I never'll be cured of my graneness!"

LOVE IN THE KITCHEN.

PELEG ARKWRIGHT.

" Now, Mr. Malone, whin yer spakin' like that,
  It is aisy to see—   Arrah, git out o' that!
Whin discoorsin' wid ladies politeness should tache
That ye're not to use hands, sir, instid ov yer spache.
Should the missus come down, sir, how would I appear
Wid me hair all bewildhered ?"

                    " Oh, Kitty, me dear,
Yer pardon I ax, but yer mouth is so sweet,
It's a betther acquaintance I'm seekin' wid it;
An' I love you so fondly—begorra, it's thrue!
That I'm always unaisy unless I'm wid you,
An' thin I'm unaisy as bad as before,
An' there's nothin'll aise me at all any more,
Until yer betrothal I've got, and bedad,
I'll not let ye go till yer promise I've had."

" It is just like yer impidence, Mr. Malone!"

" Ye can't call it impidint, Kitty, ohone,
Fur a man to be lovin' the likes of yerself:
An' ye might marry worse, if I say it meself,
Fur me heart is yer own an' me wages is good.
An' I know of a brick cabin built out ov wood,
To be had fur the askin' of Dennis McCue;
Fur he's goin' to lave it, and thin it'll do,
Wid some fixin' an' mendin' to keep out the air,
An' a bit ov a boord to patch up here an' there,
An' a thrifle ov mud to discourage the cracks—
An' we'll make up in lovin' whatever it lacks;

An' it's built on a rock, with a mighty fine view
Ov the counthry surroundin' that same avinew;
An' to be quite ginteel an extinsion we'll rig,
Convaynient for keepin' an illegant pig;
An' thin we'll both prosper as nate as ye plaze,
An' ye'll see me an' aldherman some o' those days;
And the childher will grow up with schoolin' an' sich,
An' in politics thin they'll be sure to get rich—
Oh, this is the land fur improvin' the race!
So, Kitty, mavourneen, turn round yer dear face,
An' give us one kiss the betrothal to own."

" The divil a bit ov it, Teddy Malone!
D'ye think I'd be lavin' a house ov brown stone
Fur the tumble-down shanty yer talkin' about,
While I live like a lady, wid two evenin's out,
An' a wardrobe I flatter meself is complete?
Sure ye couldn't tell missus from me on the sthreet.
An' at home it's the same, fur she's fond of her aise,
An' ye couldn't say which ov us bosses the place;
An' it's like yer asshurance to ask me to lave,
An' be the same token—now will ye behave?
Let go ov me hand, sir!"

                    " But, Kitty, me dear,
Ye can't be intindin' to always live here,
Wid niver a husband, but mopin' alone,
An' niver a baby—"

                    " Whisht, Mr. Malone!
Yer very onmannerly."

                    " Divil a wan!
It's only the truth that I'm tellin', indade,
That yer niver intindin' to die an' old maid."

" It's right ye are, Teddy, how could ye know this?"

" Well, thin, will it plaze ye to give me the kiss?"

" Get out wid yer blarney! shure how can I tell
But there might be another would suit me as well?"

" Arrah, Kitty, me darlin', don't say that agin,
If ye wouldn't be killin' the thruest of min

But if there's another ye like more than me,
Then it's faithless ye are an' its goin' I'll be,
An' I'll die broken-hearted fur lack ov the joy
That I thought to be gainin'."

           " Why, Teddy, me boy,
Is it dyin' yur talkin' ov?   What would I do—
An onmarried widda in mournin' fur you?
An' ye wanted a kiss, sir?   Well, there, if you must—
Oh, murdher, the man is devourin' me just!
Is it atin' me up ye'd be afther belike?
Well, it's not so onplaizin', ye may if ye like;
An' if any one's askin' about ye I'll own
That a broth of a boy is me Teddy Malone."

THE MATRIMONIAL ADVENTURES OF DICK MACNAMARA.

W. H. MAXWELL.

Adapted from "Hector O'Halloran."

It was the summer after the great election—and that was in the year ninety-one—an' a fine evening it was. At that time care was far from my heart, and I was taking a dance in the barn with Mary Regan, my lady's maid, when out comes Sir Thomas's own man to say that I was wanted in the parlor. " Run, bad luck to ye," says he, " and I'll finish the jig for ye! Arrah, make haste, man! Some etarnal villin has slipt a paper under the gate, and the ould master's fit to be tied. I never saw him so mad since he was chased home from Galway." Away I goes, and when I got into the parlor, there I found Sir Thomas, God rest his soul! Father Pat Butler, the parish priest, and the driver, Izzy Blake.

Sir Thomas was sittin' in the big armed chair he always sate in. He wasn't to say much the worse for licker; but it was aisy to persave that he had been lookin' at somebody that was drinkin'. The priest, och! what a head he had! was cool as a cowcumber, and only Izzy's nose was a deeper purple than when he sate down, you wouldn't know he had a drop in. It was quite plain the party were in trouble; for, to smother grief, the ould master had slipped a second glass of poteen into his tumbler just as I came in.

"Aisy, Sir Thomas!—drink aisy!" said the priest. "The whisky's killin' ye by inches!"

"Arrah, balderdash! Pat Butler, won't you let me take the color of death off the water, man, and me threatened with the gout? It's the law that's fairly murderin' me. Bad luck attend all consarned with the same! At the blast of the mail horn my heart bates like a bird; for within the last two years I have got as many lattitats by post as would paper the drawin'-room. Shemus Rhua," says he, turning to me, "did ye see a black-lookin' thief about the place when ye were hunting the young setters on the moor?"

"Arrah, Sir Thomas, if I did, don't you think I would have been after askin' him what he was doin' there?"

"Sibby Byrn saw him thrust these murthering papers under the gate, and then cut over the bog as if the divil was at his heels. Well, small blame to him for runnin'— for, by all that's beautiful, if I had gripped him, he would have gone back to the villain that employs him, lighter by both lugs. Sit down, Shemus. Izzy Blake, fill the boy a glass." And then he began, poor ould gentleman, askin' me about the dogs; but before I could answer him he gave a sigh. "Arrah," says he, "what need I be talkin' about dogs, when, after November next, the divil a four-footed baste will be left upon Killcrogher, good nor bad!"

"Something must be done immediately," said the priest. "If they foreclose the mortgage and get a resaver on the estate, we're done for."

"If we could only raise five thousand to pay that cursed claim, we might stave off the other things till some good luck would turn up," said the driver.

Sir Thomas sighed. Troth, an enemy would have pitied him!

"Arrah," says I, "hould up, Sir Thomas—who knows but we'll get to the sunny side of the hedge yet? There's Master Dick—and if he would only marry an heiress—"

"Bedad," says the ould gentleman, "Father Pat, there's sense in that."

The priest shook his head.

"And why shouldn't he?" says Sir Thomas.

"Because," returned the priest, "he's never out of one scrape till he's into another. And then he's so captious, if he was in heaven—where the Lord send him in proper time, if possible!—why, he would pick a quarrel with St. Peter."

"It's all a flow of spirits," says the ould man.

"*It's a flow of spirits* that causes it generally," says the priest; "but it's all your own fault, Sir Thomas, and I often tould ye so. Instead of lettin' him stick to his larnin', ye would have him brought up your own way, ridin' three times a week to the Clonsallagh hounds, and shooting at chalked men on the barn door through the remainder."

"Arrah, be quiet," says the ould gentleman. "Though he's my son—at least I have his mother's word for it—is there a nater horseman within the Shannon? Put Dick Macnamara on the pig-skin with anything dacent anunder him, and I'll back him over a sportin' country for all I'm worth in the world."

"Ay," said the priest, in a side-whisper; "and if ye lost, the divil a much the winner would be the better."

"He's six feet in his stockings—sound as a bell—he'll throw any man of his inches in the province, and dance the *pater-o-pee* afterwards."

"Arrah," says the priest, "if there's no way of payin' the mortgage but by dancin' the *pater-o-pee*, out we bundle in November."

"And why shouldn't he marry an heiress?" says the ould man.

"First," says Father Butler, "because he has no luck;

and second, because he has no larnin'. Wasn't I returnin'
from a sick-call only yesterday, and as God's goodness
would have it, didn't I meet my Lady French's messenger
with a note?—'Who's that from?' says I. 'Mr. Dick
Macnamara,' says he. Well, I had a misdoubtin' about
it, and so I opens the note—and—*Mona-sin-dhiaoul!*—
Lord forgive me for sayin' so!—if he hadn't spelt ' compliments' with a K!"

" And if he spelt it with two K's," says the ould gentleman, " will that hinder him marryin' a woman if she wants
a husband? I tell ye what, there's more sense in what
Shemus Rhua says than any of ye seems to know. Wasn't
the family as badly off when my grandfather—God rest
his soul!—ran away with Miss Kelly?"

" And where will you get a Miss Kelly nowadays? It's
not out of every bush you'll kick a lady, lame of a leg, and
twenty thousand down upon the nail!"

" What was she the worse for that?" says Sir Thomas.
" Don't ye mind what my grandfather said to Lord Castle-
town the week after. 'Didn't I,' says my grandfather,
' manage the matter well, my lord?' ' Ye did in troth,
Ulic—and ye made a grate hit of it, if ye'r amiable lady
was only right upon the pins.' ' Well, my lord,' says he—
' what the divil matter if she is a wee bit lame? Does
your lordship suppose that men marry wives to run races
with them?'"

Well, there's no use makin' a long story about it. At
Killcrogher things couldn't be worse than they were; and
when we had finished a second bottle of poteen, we all
agreed that the divil a chance, good, bad or indifferent,
was left but for Dick Macnamara to marry a wife with a
fortune—and with or without a spavin—just as the Lord
would direct it.

This was all mighty well, but where was the lady to be
found? Of heiresses there was no scarcity in Galway, if
their own story was but true; but then their fortunes

were so well secured, that nather principal nor interest could be got at.

"England's the place," says the ould master. "Dick would get twenty thousand for the askin'."

"And how is he to go there?" says the priest. "He must travel like a gentleman, or they wouldn't touch him with a tent-pole—and where's the money for that?"

"Let Izzy drive the tenants."

"Arrah, Sir Thomas! it's aisy talkin'—the divil a pound I could drive out of them to save your life. *Mona-sin-dhiaoul!* ye might as well expect blood from a turnip, or to borrow knee-buckles off a Hielanman."

Well, we were fairly nonplushed for a time, but we got matters right afterwards. The ould ladies, the master's sisters, had a trifle by them, if anybody could manage to get at it. Well, the priest put it to them, for the glory of God, and Sir Thomas for the honor of the family. They came down at last, and, between them, for a hundred. Sir Thomas lent us his own pistols, and Izzy Blake passed his word in Galway for the clothes.

On the strength of Izzy we taught book-keeping to a tailor. His name, I mind, was Jerry Riley—and I fancy we're in his ledger to this day.

I'll never forget the mornin' we started. We set out at six o'clock, as we had to ride to Moylough to catch the Tuam mail. Every soul in Killcrogher was astir, and waitin' at door or windy to see us off—some givin' their blessin', and others their good advice.

"Mind yer eye, Dick!" said the ould gentleman from the parlor.

"Don't take anything but what's ready," cried the priest from the hall door.

"Remember, you're of the Coolavins by the mother's side," called my lady from her bedroom; "so look to blood as well as suet, Dick."

"The money—the money," cried the priest.

" Dick, dear, ye're on book-oath to me !" whispered Mary Regan, as we passed her.

" Don't be quarreling about trifles," said the priest.

" Nor let anybody tramp upon your corn, for all that," cried Sir Thomas.

" The money—the money, Dick—and that's the last words of yer clargy," roared the priest.

" Don't miss mass, if you can," screamed the ould ladies from the lobby.

" Nor the money !" and father Butler signed his blessing after us as we rode away.

" Stop ! stop !" roared the ould master. " Another word, and God keep ye, Dick ! Always fight with ye'r back to the sun. Drink slow—don't mix ye'r licker, nor sit with ye'r back to the fire—and the divil won't put ye under the table !"

These were the last words we heard—the gatekeeper's wife flung an ould shoe after us for luck—and away we went to make our fortune.

When we reached Moylough, the coach was standin' before the door of the hotel, for the passengers had gone in to breakfast, and by the time we had taken the dust out of our throats with a throw at the counter, the company had come out again. Two or three of them roofed it like myself, and one lady, with blue feathers and a yalla pelisse, stepped inside. She was a clipper ! and there was enough of her into the bargain. As Master Dick traveled like a raal gentleman, of coorse he hopped in too.

Well, when we stopped to change horses, Dick and the lady were thick as inkle-wavers. " Shemus," says he, " bring out a glass of sherry, and a drop of water in the bottom of a tumbler, with a sketch of sperits through it." They drank genteelly to each other, and away we rowled again. Indeed, at every stop the same order was repeated. The lady was comin' from the say, and that made her dry, I suppose, and from the time he was a boy, Dick Macnamara had an unquenchable thirst upon him.

We reached Athlone in the evening, and stopped at the Red Lion. Dick handed out the lady with the yalla pelisse, and ye would have thought they would have shaken each other's hands off. Well, a maid-sarvant took her bandbox—Dick gave her the arm—away they flourished together—and I stayed at the inn door to see the luggage safe off the coach.

Before long the young master returned.

"Shemus," says he, shuttin' the door behind him, "isn't Miss Callaghan a spanker?"

"'Pon my soul, she's a cliver girl, with fine action," says I.

"Bad luck to ye!" said he, "ye talk of her as ye would of a horse. But, Shemus, I thought as we were all alone, I would try if I could put my *comether* over her by the way of practice. Och! if she was only an heiress! When I kissed her at partin' in the hall, she tould me she could follow me over the world."

Well, afther we had supper, Master Dick sends for me to come up-stairs; and as it was too soon to go to bed, down we sate over a hot tumbler to settle what was to be done when we got to London. Ye see, we knew that in England there were heiresses *galore*—but the thing was, how the divil were we to find them?

Well, after we had been talkin' half an hour, in comes the waiter. "Is there one Mister Macnamara here?" says he.

"That's me," Dick answers.

"Mister Callaghan's after askin' for ye," says he.

"Parade him," says Dick.

So in steps an ould gentleman, clane shaved enough, but about the clothes he had rather a shuck appearance. He bows, and Dick bows—and down sits the ould gentleman, an' draws over a tumbler.

"Ye had a pleasant journey of it, Mister Macnamara," says he, commencin' the conversation. "My daughter says that ye're the best of company. In troth she speaks large of ye."

With that they drinks one another's health—an' from one thing they comes on to another. I had pulled my chair away to the corner, ye see, but Dick winked to me as much as to say, "Shemus, stay where ye are."

"An' so you're goin' to better yourself with a wife?" says the ould fellow.

"There's no denyin' it," says Dick.

"Well, 'pon my conscience, it's the best thing ivir a young man did, for it keeps him out of harm's way. An' are ye for soon changin' ye'r state?"

"Divil a use tellin' lies among friends," says Dick. "The sooner the better."

"Faith—an' it has come rather sudden upon Sophy," says Mister Callaghan. "But God's will be done! Her brother will be home in an hour. I wish there was only time to send for her mother to Roscrea."

"What's wanted with her mother?" says Dick.

"Nothin' partikler," says Mr. Callaghan, "only the ould lady would like to see her little girl married."

"An' when is she to be married?" inquired Dick.

"Why, as there seems to be a hurry," replies the ould fellow, "it may as well be done ' out of the face.' "

"An' if it wouldn't be an impertinent question," says Dick, "arrah! who's to be the happy man?"

"An' are ye jokin'?" says ould Callaghan. "Arrah, who should it be but yourself?"

"Myself?" says Dick. "Shemus," says he—"the divil an appearance of licker's on the ould man; what does he mane at all?"

"Of coorse," says I, "that ye're goin' to marry his daughter."

"Exactly," cried ould Callaghan.

"If she's not married till she marries me, she'll be single for a month of Sundays," says Dick.

Up jumps the ould fellow in a rage—and up jumps Dick Macnamara—and then such fendin' and provin' and such racketing through the room—till out rushed Mister Callaghan, swarin' he would be revenged before he slept.

When he slammed to the door, I turns round to Dick, to ask what it was all about.

"Arrah, the divil have them that knows," says he; "I just coorted a little bit with the girl as we were alone in the coach, by the way of bringin' my han' in before we got to England."

"Be my soul," says I, "ye've made a nate kettle of fish of it!—Arrah, Dick, *avourneeine*—ar'n't ye in the centre of a hobble—coortin's one thing, and marryin's another. Wouldn't the priest be proud of ye to go back with Miss Callaghan under yer arm?—and with about as much money as would pay turnpike for a walking stick."

Feaks, things looked but quare the more we considered them; so we thought we would order a chaise, push on to Moate, and lave Sophy Callaghan to her own amiable family, as she was too valuable for us. But, as matters turned up, we wer'n't allowed to set off as aisy as we intended. Before the chaise could come round, we heard feet upon the stairs, and the door opens, and in comes five as loose lookin' lads as ye would meet in a day's walk. They were all fresh as if they had been hard at the drinkin'—and they were bent on mischief—for the second fellow had a twist in the eye, and a pistol-case under his arm.

"Mister Macnamara," says the first, "my name's Callaghan. There's no use for any rigmarole, as the light's goin' fast, so I just stepped in to ask you consarnin' your intentions towards my sister Sophy."

"The divil an intention have I, good or bad, about ye'r sister Sophy," replied Dick, as stiff as a churchwarden.

"Then ye can be at no loss to guess the consequence?"

"Feaks, an' I am," says Dick; "as I'm no conjurer."

" If ye don't marry her within an hour," says he, " I'll be after sayin' something disagreeable."

" I'll not keep ye in suspense half the time," replied Dick.

" Then ye'll marry her ?" says he.

" You were nivir more astray," replied Dick, " since ye were born."

" Then I'll trouble ye for satisfaction," says he.

" With all my heart," says Dick.

" What time in the mornin'," said the other, " would fit ye'r convanience ?"

" We're rather in a hurry," says Dick, pointin' to the post-chay that had come round, and on which the hostler was tyin' the traps; " to-night would be a great accommodation, if it was the same to you."

" Ye can't do better," says one of the others, " than step up to the ball-room. There's good light still, and the room's long enough."

Be gogstay ! Dick Macnamara closed with the offer like a man. I was sent for the pistols, and the gentlemen called for a bottle of sherry. You see, in case of accident, it would come well before a jury that they drank each other's healths, and fought in perfect friendship, for that would benefit the survivor.

They slipped into the ball-room, and everybody thought the thing was settled, they were so quiet and civil with each other as they went up-stairs. The pistols were charged—" An' now," says Callaghan, " for the last time, I ask ye, will ye have my sister Sophy ?"

" Arrah, don't lose the light in talkin'—ye have my answer already," says Dick Macnamara.

Well, they were placed in the corners of the room, and a man with a red nose asked " if they were ready !" both said " Yes !" " Fire !" says he. Slap off went both pistols like the clapping of a hand, and down dropped Mr. Callaghan with a ball clane into his calf. Well, everybody

ran to lift him, when suddenly the cry of murder was raised
from the other end of the room, and out dashed a man in a
shirt and scarlet night-cap, and a fat woman close at his
heels, just as they had tumbled out of bed.

"Oh, Holy Moses!" says he. "Save our lives! Murder! Murder!"

"What's wrong with ye, honest man?" says I.

"Give us time for repentince!" says she, droppin' on her
knees. "We're dalers in soft goods, and obliged to tell
lies in the way of bisnis."

"For shame," says I, "for a dacent young woman to
come before company in that way! Arrah, put the petticoat on ye at least." Troth, it was no wonder the cratures
were scared. Ye see, there was a closet off the ball-room,
divided with a wooden partition; and as the house was
full, and the travelers tired, they stuck them into it for
the night. Divil a one of us, in the hurry, thought of
lookin' in; and when the man woke with the noise, and
sate up to listen what the matter was, the fellow with the
red nose cried "Fire!" and Callaghan's ball pops through
the partition, and whips the tassel off the daler's night-
cap.

Well, for fear of any fresh shindy, I got the luggage tied
upon the shay. Dick shook hands with Callaghan, and
sent his compliments to his sister Sophy, and away we
drove to Moate; and the next evening got safe to Dublin.

TEDDY O'TOOLE'S SIX BULLS.

A merry evening party in an English country town
were bantering poor Teddy O'Toole, the Irishman, about
his countrymen being so famous for bulls.

"By my faith," said Teddy, "you needn't talk about
that same in this place; you're as fond of bulls as any
people in all the world, so you are."

"Nonsense!" some of the party replied; "how do you make that out?"

"Why, sure, it's very aisy, it is; for in this paltry bit of a town you've got more public houses nor I ever seen wid the sign of the bull over the doors, so you have," said Teddy.

"Nay, Teddy, very few of those; but there's some of 'em, you know, in every town."

"Yes," said Teddy, obstinately sticking to his text, for he had laid a trap for his friends, "but you've more nor your share, barring that you're so fond of bulls, as I say; I'm sure I can count half a dozen of 'em."

"Pooh, nonsense!" cried the party; "that will never do: what'll you bet on that, Teddy? You're out there, my boy, depend upon it; we know the town as well as you, and what will you bet?"

"Indeed, my brave boys, I'll not bet at all; I'm no better, I assure ye—I should be worse if I wur." This sally tickled his companions, and he proceeded. "But I'll be bound to name and count the six."

"Well, do, do," said several voices.

"Now, let me see; there's the Black Bull."

"Yes, that's one."

"Then, there's the Red Bull."

"That's two."

"And the White Bull."

"Come, that's three."

"And the Pied Bull."

"So there is; you'll not go much further."

"And then there's—there's—there's the Golden Bull, in ——what's it street?"

"Well done, Teddy; that's five sure enough, but you're short yet."

"Aye," said the little letter carrier, who sat smirking in the corner, "and he will be short, for there isn't one more, I know."

"And then, remember," continued Teddy, carefully pursuing his enumeration, "there's the Dun cow."

At this a burst of laughter fairly shook the room, and busy hands kept the tables and glasses rattling amidst boisterous cries of:

"A bull! a bull!"

Looking serious at all around, Teddy deliberately asked—

"Do you call that a bull?"

"To be sure it's a bull," exclaimed several voices at once.

"Then," said Teddy, "that's the sixth."

Here an unavoidable defeat in the direct was converted into a victory in the antipodean, by the cleverly obtained admission of the vanquished party themselves.

CONNOR.

"To the memory of Patrick Connor; this simple stone was erected by his fellow-workmen."

Those words you may read any day upon a white slab in a cemetery not many miles from New York; but you might read them a hundred times without guessing at the little tragedy they indicate, without knowing the humble romance which ended with the placing of that stone above the dust of one poor, humble man.

In his shabby frieze jacket and mud-laden brogans, he was scarcely an attractive object as he walked into Mr. Bawne's great tin and hardware shop one day and presented himself at the counter with an—

"I've been tould ye advertised for hands, yer honor."

"Fully supplied, my man," said Mr. Bawne, not lifting his head from his account book.

"I'd work faithfully, sir, and take low wages, till I could do better, and I'd learn—I would that."

It was an Irish brogue, and Mr. Bawne always declared that he never would employ an incompetent hand.

Yet the tone attracted him. He turned briskly, and with his pen behind his ear, addressed the man, who was only one of fifty who had answered his advertisement for four workmen that morning.

" What makes you expect to learn faster than other folks—are you any smarter ?"

" I'll not say that," said the man, " but I'd be wishing to ; and that would make it aisier."

" Are you used to the work ?"

" I've done a bit of it."

" Much ?"

" No, yer honor. I'll tell no lie; Tim O'Toole hadn't the like of this place ; but I know a bit about tins."

" You are too old for an apprentice, and you'd be in the way, I calculate," said Mr. Bawne, looking at the brawny arms and bright eyes that promised strength and intelligence. " Besides, I know your countrymen—lazy, good-for-nothing fellows, who never do their best. No, I've been taken in by Irish hands before, and I won't have another."

" The Virgin will have to be after bringing them over to me in her two arms, thin," said the man, despairingly, " for I've tramped all the day for the last fortnight, and niver a job can I get, and that's the last penny I have, yer honor, and it's but a half one."

As he spoke he spread his palm open, with an English half-penny in it.

" Bring whom over ?" asked Mr. Bawne, arrested by the odd speech, as he turned upon his heel and turned back again.

" Jist Nora and Jamesy."

" Who are they ?"

" The wan's me wife, the other me child," said the man. " O, masther, just thry me. How'll I bring 'em over to me, if no one will give me a job ? I want to be airning, and

the whole big city seems against it, and me with arms like
them!" He bared his arms to the shoulder as he
spoke, and Mr. Bawne looked at them, and then at his face.

"I'll hire you for a week," he said; "and now as it's
noon, go down to the kitchen and tell the girl to get you
some dinner—a hungry man can't work."

With an Irish blessing, the new hand obeyed, while Mr.
Bawne, untying his apron, went up-stairs to his own meal.
Suspicious as he was of the new hand's integrity and
ability, he was agreeably disappointed. Connor worked
hard, and actually learned fast. At the end of the week
he was engaged permanently, and soon was the best workman in the shop."

He was a great talker, but not fond of drink or wasting
money. As his wages grew, he hoarded every penny, and
wore the same shabby clothes in which he had made his
first appearance.

"Beer costs money," he said one day, "and ivery cint
I spind puts off the bringing Nora and Jamesy over; and
as for clothes, them I have must do me. Better no coat
to my back than no wife and boy by my fireside; and
anyhow, it's slow work saving."

It was slow work, but he kept at it all the same. Other
men, thoughtless and full of fun, tried to make him drink;
made a jest of his saving habits, coaxed him to accompany
them to places of amusement, or to share in their Sunday
frolics.

All in vain. Connor liked beer, liked fun, liked com-
panionship; but he would not delay that long-looked-for
bringing of Nora over, and was not "mane enough" to
accept favor of others. He kept his way, a martyr to his
one great wish, living on little, working at night on any
extra job that he could earn a few shillings by, running
errands in his noon-tide hours of rest, and talking to any
one who would listen to him of his one great hope, and
of Nora and little Jamesy.

At first the men, who prided themselves on being all Americans, and on turning out the best work in the city, made a sort of butt of Connor, whose wild Irish ways and verdancy were indeed often laughable. But he won their hearts at last, and one day, mounting a work-bench, he shook his little bundle, wrapped in a red handkerchief, before their eyes, and shouted, " Look, boys ; I've got the whole at last! I'm going to bring Nora and Jamesy over at last! Whorooo!! I've got it at last!!!" All felt sympathy in his joy, and each grasped his great hand in cordial congratulations, and one proposed to treat all round, and drink a good voyage to Nora.

They parted in a merry mood, most of the men going to comfortable homes. But poor Connor's resting-place was a poor lodging-house, where he shared a crazy garret with four other men, and in the joy of his heart the poor fellow exhibited his handkerchief, with his hard-earned savings tied up in a wad in the middle, before he put it under his pillow and fell asleep.

When he awakened in the morning, he found his treasure gone ; some villain, more contemptible than most bad men, had robbed him.

At first Connor could not even believe it lost. He searched every corner of the room, shook his quilt and blankets, and begged those about him " to quit joking, and give it back."

But at last he realized the truth.

" Is any man that bad that it's thaved from me ?" he asked, in a breathless way. " Boys, is any man that bad?" And some one answered : " No doubt of it, Connor; it's sthole."

Then Connor put his head down on his hands and lifted up his voice and wept. It was one of those sights which men never forget. It seemed more than he could bear, to have Nora and his child " put," as he expressed it, " months away from him again."

But when he went to work that day it seemed to all who saw him that he had picked up a new determination. His hands were never idle. His face seemed to say, "I'll have Nora with me yet."

At noon he scratched out a letter, blotted and very strangely scrawled, telling Nora what had happened; and those who observed him noticed that he had no meat with his dinner. Indeed from that moment he lived on bread, potatoes and cold water, and worked as few men ever worked before. It grew to be the talk of the shop, and now that sympathy was excited, every one wanted to help Connor. Jobs were thrown in his way, kind words and friendly wishes helped him mightily; but no power could make him share the food or drink of any other workman. It seemed a sort of charity to him.

Still he was helped along. A present from Mr. Bawne at pay day set Nora, as he said, "a week nearer," and this and that and the other added to the little hoard. It grew faster than the first, and Connor's burden was not so heavy. At last, before he hoped it, he was once more able to say, "I'm going to bring them over," and to show his handkerchief in which, as before, he tied up his earnings; this time, however, only to his friends. Cautious among strangers, he hid the treasure, and kept his vest buttoned over it night and day until the tickets were bought and sent. Then every man, woman and child, capable of hearing or understanding, knew that Nora and her baby were coming.

There was John Jones, who had more of the brute in his composition than usually falls to the lot of man, would spend ten minutes of the noon hour in reading the Irish news to Connor. There was Tom Barker, the meanest man among the number, who had never been known to give anything to any one before, absolutely bartered an old jacket for a pair of gilt vases, which a peddler brought in his basket to the shop, and presented them to Connor for his Nora's mantel-piece. And here was idle Dick, the apprentice, who actually worked two hours on Connor's work when illness kept the Irishman at home one day. Connor felt this kindness, and returned it whenever it was in his power, and the days flew by and brought at last a letter from his wife.

"She would start as he desired, and she was well and so was the boy, and might the Lord bring them safely to each other's arms, and bless them who had been so kind to him." That was the substance of the epistle which Connor proudly assured his fellow-workmen Nora wrote herself. She had lived at service as a girl, with a certain good old lady, who had given her the items of an education, which Connor told upon his fingers: "The radin', that's one, and the writin', that's three, and moreover, she knows all that a woman can." Then he looked up with tears in his eyes, and asked, "Do you wondher the time seems long between me an' her, boys?"

So it was. Nora at the dawn of day—Nora at noon—Nora at night—until the news came that the "Stormy Petrel" had come to port, and Connor, breathless and pale with excitement, flung up his cap in the air and shouted.

It happened on a holiday afternoon, and half a dozen men were ready to go with Connor to the steamer and give his wife a greeting. Her little home was ready; Mr. Bawne's own servant had put it in order, and Connor took one peep at it before he started.

"She hadn't the like of that in the ould counthry," he said, "but she'll know how to keep them tidy."

Then he led the way towards the dock where the steamer lay, and at a pace that made it hard for the rest to follow him. The spot was reached at last; a crowd of vehicles blockaded the street; a troop of emigrants came thronging up; fine cabin passengers were stepping into cabs, and drivers, porters, and all manner of employees were yelling and shouting in the usual manner. Nora would wait on board for her husband; he knew that.

The little group made their way into the vessel at last, and there, amid those who sat watching for coming friends, Connor searched for the two so dear to him; patiently at first—eagerly but patiently—but by and by growing anxious and excited.

"She would never go alone," he said, "she'd be lost entirely; I bade her wait, but I don't see her, boys; I think she's not in it."

"Why don't you see the captain?" asked one, and Connor jumped at the suggestion. In a few minutes he stood before a portly, rubicund man, who nodded to him kindly.

"I am looking for my wife, yer honor," said Connor, " and I can't find her."

"Perhaps she's gone ashore," said the captain.

"I bade her wait," said Connor.

"Women don't always do as they are bid, you know," said the captain.

"Nora would," said Connor; " but maybe she was left behind. Maybe she didn't come. I somehow think she didn't."

At the name of Nora the captain started. In a moment he asked, " What is your name?"

" Pat Connor," said the man.

" And your wife's name was Nora?"

" That's her name, and the boy with her is Jamesy, yer honor," said Connor.

The captain looked at Connor's friends; they looked at the captain. Then he said huskily, " Sit down, my man; I've got something to tell you."

" She's left behind?" said Connor.

"She sailed with us," said the captain.

" Where is she?" asked Connor.

The captain made no answer.

" My man," he said, "we all have our trials; God sends them. Yes—Nora started with us."

Connor said nothing. He was looking at the captain now, white to his lips.

"It's been a sickly season," said the captain; "we have had illness on board—the cholera. You know that."

"I didn't, I can't read; they kept it from me," said Connor.

"We didn't want to frighten him," said one in a half whisper.

"You know how long we lay at Quarantine?"

"The ship I came in did that," said Connor. "Did ye say Nora went ashore? Ought I to be looking for her, captain?"

"Many died—many children," went on the captain. "When we were half way here your boy was taken sick."

"Jamesy?" gasped Connor.

"His mother watched him night and day," said the captain, "and we did all we could, but at last he died; only one of many. There were five buried that day. But it broke my heart to see the mother looking out upon the water. 'It's his father I think of,' said she, 'he's longing to see poor Jamesy.'"

Connor groaned.

"Keep up if you can, my man," said the captain. "I wish any one else had to tell it rather than I. That night Nora was taken ill also, very suddenly; she grew worse fast. In the morning she called me to her. 'Tell Connor I died thinking of him,' she said, 'and tell him to meet me.' And, my man, God help you, she never said anything more—in an hour she was gone."

Connor had risen. He stood up, trying to steady himself; looking at the captain with his eyes dry as two stones. Then he turned to his friends.

"I've got my death, boys," he said, and then dropped to the deck like a log.

They raised him and bore him away. In an hour he was at home on the little bed which had been made ready

for Nora, weary with her long voyage. There at last he
opened his eyes. Old Mr. Bawne bent over him; he had
been summoned by the news, and the room was full of
Connor's fellow-workmen.

"Better, Connor?" asked the old man.

"A dale," said Connor, "it's aisy now; I'll be with her
soon. And look ye, masther, I've learnt one thing—God
is good; He wouldn't let me bring Nora over to me, but
he's takin' me over to her and Jamesy, over the river;
don't you see it, and her standin' on the other side to welcome me?"

And with these words Connor stretched out his arms.
Perhaps he did see Nora—Heaven only knows—and so
died.

THE FIGHT OF HELL-KETTLE.

TYRONE POWER.

Never let it be said the days of chivalry are fled; her-
alds may have ceased to record good blows stricken, to
the tune of a "largesse worthie knights,"—pennon and
banner, square and swallow-tail'd sleeve and scarf, with
all the trumpery of chivalry, are long since dead, 'tis true;
but the lofty, generous feeling with which that term has
become synonymous, is yet burning clear and bright within
ten thousand bosoms, not one of which ever throbbed at
the recollections which the word itself inspires in "gentil
heartes," or could tell the difference between Or and
Gules, or Vert and Sable, as the following narration of a
combat between two "churles," or "villains," as the herald would term my worthies, will, I trust, go nigh to prove.

It was the fair night at Donard, a small village in the
very heart of the mountains of Wicklow, when at the turn
of a corner leading out of the Dunlavin road, towards the
middle of the fair, two ancient foemen abruptly encountered.

They eyed one another for a moment without moving a step, when the youngest, a huge six-foot mountaineer, in a long top-coat, having his shirt open from breast to ear, displaying on the least movement a brawny chest that was hairy enough for a trunk, growing rather impatient, said in a quick under-tone, that a listener would have set down for the extreme of politeness:

"You'll lave the wall, Johnny Evans?"

To which civil request came reply, in a tone equally bland:

"Not at your biddin', if you stand there till next fair day, Mat Dolan."

"You know well I could fling you neck and heels into that gutter, in one minute, Johnny, me bouchil."

"You might, indeed, if you call up twenty of the Dunlavin faction at your back," coolly replied Evans.

"I mane, here's the two empty hands could do all that, and never ax help, 'ather," retorted Dolan, thrusting forth two huge paws from under his coat.

"In the name o' heaven, thin thry it," said Evans, flinging the shillelagh he had up to this time been balancing curiously, over the roof of the cottage by which they stood; adding, "here's a pair of fists, with as little in thim as your own!"

"It's aisy to brag by your own barn, Johnny Evans," said Dolan, pointing with a sneer to the police guard-house, on the opposite side of the way, a hundred yards lower down; the peelers would not be likely to look on, and see a black Orangeman, like yourself, quilted in his own town, under their noses, by one Mat Dolan, from Dunlavin, all the way."

"There's raison in that, any way, Matty," replied John, glancing in the direction indicated. "It's not likely thim that's paid by government to keep the peace, would stand by and see it broke, by Papist or Protestant; but I'll make a bargain wid you; if your blood's over-hot for your skin—

which I think, to say the truth, it has long been—come off
at once to Hell-kettle wid me, and in the light of this
blessed moon I'll fight it out wid you, toe to toe ; and we'll
both be aisier after, whichever's bate."

" There's my hand to that, at a word, Johnny," cried
Dolan, suiting the action to the word—and the hands of
the foes clasped freely and frankly together.

" But are we to be only ourselves, do ye mane ?" inquired
Matthew.

" And enuff, too," answered Evans ; " we couldn't pick
a friend out of any tint above, without raising a hulabaloo
the divil wou'dn't quiet without blows.   Here, now, I'll
give you the wall, only you jump the hedge into Charles
Faucett's meadow, and cut across the hill by Holy-well
into the road, where you'll meet me; divil a soul else
you'll meet that way to-night; and I want to call at home
for the tools."

" Keep the wall," cried Dolan, as Evans stepped aside,
springing himself at the same time into the road, ankle-
deep in mud ; " I'll wait for you at the bridge, on the
Holy-wood glin road.   Good-by."

A moment after, Dolan had cleared the hedge leading
out of the lands into Mr. Faucett's paddock, and Evans
was quietly plodding his way homeward.   To reach his
cottage, he had to run the gauntlet through the very
throng of the fair, amidst the crowded tents, whence re-
sounded the ill-according sounds of the bagpipe and fid-
dle, and the loud whoo! of the jig dancers, as they beat
with active feet the temporary floor, that rattled with their
tread.   Johnny made short greetings with those of his
friends he encountered, and on entering his house, plucked
a couple of black, business-like looking sticks from the
chimney, hefted them carefully, and measured them together with an eye as strict as ever gallant paired rapier
with, till, satisfied of their equality, he put his top-coat
over his shoulders, and departing by the back door, rapidly

cleared two or three small gardens, and made at once for the fields. As Dolan dropped from the high bank into the lane near the bridge on one side, Evans leapt the gate opposite.

"You've lost no time, fegs," observed Matthew, as they drew together, shoulder to shoulder, stalking rapidly on.

"I've been vexed to keep you waiting, this time, anyhow," replied Johnny, and few other words passed.

Just beyond the bridge they left the road together, and mounting the course of the little stream, in a few minutes were shut out from the possibility of observance in a wild, narrow glen, at whose head was a waterfall of some eighteen feet. The pool which received this little cascade was exceeding deep, and having but one narrow outlet between the huge stones, the pent waters were forced round and round, boiling and chafing for release; and hence the not unpoetic name of Hell-kettle given to this spot. The ground immediately about it was wild, bare and stony, and in no way derogated from this fearful title.

Near the fall is a little platform or level of some twenty yards square, the place designed by Evans for the battleground. Arrived here, the parties halted; and as Dolan stooped to raise a little of the pure stream in his hand to his lips, Evans cast his coats and vest on the gray stone close by, and pulling his shirt over his head, stood armed for the fight, not so heavy or tall a man as his antagonist Dolan, but wiry as a terrier, and having, in his agility and training, advantages that more than balanced the difference of weight and age.

"I've been thinking, Johnny Evans," cried Dolan, as he leisurely stripped in turn, "we must have two thrys, after all, to show who's the best man; you have got the alpeens wid you, I see, and I'm not the boy to say no to thim, but I expect you'll ha' the best ind o' the stick, for it's well known there is not your match in Wicklow, if there is in Wexford itself."

"That day's past, Matty Dolan," replied Evans. "It's

five years since you and me had bad words, at the Pattern o' the Seven-churches, and that was the last stroke I struck with a stick. There's eight years betune our ages, and you're the heavier man by two stone or near it ; what more 'ud yez have, man alive ?"

" Oh, never fear me, John, we'll never split about trifles," quietly replied Dolan ; " but, see here, let's dress one another, as they do potatoes, both ways. Stand fairly up to me for half a dozen rounds, fist to fist, and I'll hould the alpeen till you're tired after id."

"Why, look here, Matty, you worked over-long on George's Quay, and were over-friendly with the great boxer, Mister Donolan, for me to be able for yez wid the fists," cried Evans. "But we'll split the difference; I'll give you a quarter of an hour out o' me wid the fists, and you'll give the same time, if I'm able, with the alpeen after ; and we'll toss head or harp, which comes first."

Evans turned a copper flat on the back of his hand, as he ended his proposal, and in the same moment Dolan cried :

" Harp forever."

" Harp it is," echoed Evans, holding the coin up in the moon's ray, which shone out but fitfully as dark clouds kept slowly passing over her cold face.

In the next moment they were toe to toe, in the centre of the little plain, both looking determined and confident ; though an amateur would have at once decided in favor of Dolan's pose.

To describe the fight scientifically would be too long an affair ; suffice it, that although Johnny's agility gave him the best of a couple of severe falls, yet his antagonist's straight hitting and superior weight left him the thing hollow : till five quick rounds left Evans deaf to time and tune, and as sick as though he had swallowed a glass of antimonial wine instead of poteen.

Dolan carried his senseless foe to the pool and dashed water over him by the hatful.

" Look at my watch," was Johnny's first word, on gaining breath.

" I can't tell the time by watch," cried Dolan, a little sheepish.

" Give it here, man," cried Johnny, adding, as he rubbed his left eye, the other being fast closed, " by the Boyne, this is the longest quarter of an hour I ever knew—it wants three minutes yet," and as he spoke, again he rose up before his man.

" Sit still, Johnny," exclaimed Matthew; "I'll forgive you the three minutes, any how."

" Well, thank ye for that," said Johnny : " I wish I may be able to return the compliment presently; but by St. Donagh, I've mighty little concait left in myself, just now."

Within five minutes, armed with the well-seasoned twigs Johnny had brought with him, those honest fellows again stood front to front, and although Evans had lost much of the elasticity of carriage which had ever been his characteristic when the alpeen was in his hand and the shamrock under his foot, in times past; although his left eye was closed, and the whole of that side of his physiognomy was swollen and disfigured through the mauling he had received at the hands of Dolan, who opposed him to all appearance fresh as at the first, yet was his confidence in himself unshaken, and in the twinkling of his right eye, a close observer might have read a sure anticipation of the victory a contest of five minutes gave to him, for it was full that time before Johnny struck a good-will blow, and when it took effect, a second was uncalled for. The point of the stick had caught Dolan fairly on the right temple, and laying open the whole of the face down to the chin, as if done by a sabre stroke, felling him senseless.

After some attempts at recalling his antagonist to perception by the brookside without success, Evans began to feel a little alarmed for his life, and hoisting him on his

back, retraced his steps to the village, without ever halt-
ing by the way, and bore his insensible burthen into the
first house he came to, where, as the devil would have it, a
sister of Dolan's was sitting, having a goster with the
owner, one widow Donnevan, over a rakin' pot o' tay.

" God save all here," said Johnny, crossing the floor without ceremony, and depositing Mat on the widow's bed,
" Wid'y, by your lave, let Mat Dolan lie quiet here a bit,
till I run down-town for the doctor."

" Dolan !" screamed the sister and the widow in a breath,
" Mat, is it Mat Dolan that's lying a corse here, and I, his
own sister, not to know he was in trouble ?"

Loud and long were the lamentations that followed this
unlucky discovery. The sister rushed franticly out into
the middle of the road, screaming and calling on the friends
of Dolan to revenge his murder on Evans and the Orange-
men that had decoyed and slain him. The words passed
from lip to lip, soon reaching down to the heart of the fair,
where most of the parties were about this time corn'd for
anything.

" Johnny Evans," cried the widow Donnevan, as he
made, in few words, the story known to her, " true or not
true, this is no place for you now ; the whole of his faction
will be up here in a minute, and you will be killed like a
dog on the flure ; out wid you, and down to the guard-
house while the coast's clear."

" I'd best, maybe," cried Evans ; "and I'll send the
doctor up the quicker—but mind, widow—if that boy ever
spakes, he'll say a fairer fight was never fought—get that
out of him for the love o' heaven, Mrs. Donnevan."

" He hasn't a word in him, I fear," cried the widow, as
Johnny left the door, and with the readiness of her sex,
assisted by one or two elderly gossips, who were by this
time called in, she bathed the wounds with spirits, and
used every device which much experience in cracked
crowns, acquired during the lifetime of Willy Donnevan,

her departed lord, suggested to her. Meantime Evans, whilst making his way down through the village, had been met and recognized by the half-frantic sister of Dolan and her infuriated friends, who had been all for some time puzzled at the absence of him who was proverbial as

> " Best foot on the flure,
> First stick in the fight."

" There's the murderer of Mat Dolan, boys," cried the woman, as some ten or twelve yards off she recognized Johnny, who was conspicuous enough, wearing his shirt like a herald's tabard as in his haste he had drawn it on at Hell-kettle. With a yell that might have scared the devil, thirty athletic fellows sprang forward at full speed after Evans, who wisely never staid to remonstrate, but made one pair of heels serve, where the hands of Briareus, had he possessed as many, would not have availed him. He arrived at Mrs. Donnevan's door before his pursuers; he raised the latch, but it gave no way; the bar was drawn within, and had his strength been equal to it, further fight was become impracticable—turning with his back to the door, there stood Johnny, like a lion at bay, uttering no word, since he well knew that words would not prevail against the fury of his foes. Forward with wild cries and loud imprecations rushed the foremost of the pursuers, and Evans' life was not worth one moment's purchase; a dozen sticks already clattered like hail upon his guard, and on the wall over his head, when the door suddenly opened inwards, back tumbled Johnny, and into the space he thus left vacant stepped a gaunt figure, naked to the waist, pale and marked with a stream of blood yet flowing from the temple. With wild cries the mob pressed back.

"It's a ghost! it's Dolan's ghost!" shouted twenty voices, above all of which was heard that of the presumed spirit, crying in good Irish, " That's a lie, boys, it's Mat Dolan himself! able and willing to make a ghost of the first man that lifts a hand agin Johnny Evans; who bate

me at Hell-kettle like a man and bro't me here after, on
his back, like a brother."

"Was it a true fight, Mat?" demanded one or two of the
foremost, recovering confidence enough to approach Dolan,
who, faint from the exertion he had made, was now resting
his head against the doorpost.

A pause, and the silence of death followed. The brows
of the men began to darken, as they drew close to Dolan.
Evans saw his life depended on the reply of his antagonist,
who already seemed lapsed into insensibility.

"Answer, Mat Dolan!" he cried impressively, "for the
love of heaven, answer me—was it a true fight?"

The voice appeared to rouse the fainting man. He
raised himself in the doorway, and stretched his right
hand towards Evans, exclaiming:

"True as the cross, by the blessed Virgin!" and as he
spoke, fell back into the arms of his friends.

Evans was now safe. Half a dozen of the soberest of
the party escorted him down to the police station, where
they knew he would be secure; and Dolan's friends, bearing him with them on a car, departed, without attempting
any riot or retaliation.

This chance took place sixteen years ago; but since that
day there never was a fair at Dunlavin that the Orangeman Evans was not the guest of Dolan; nor is there a fair-
night at Donard that Mat Dolan does not pass under the
humble roof of Johnny Evans. I give the tale as it
occurred, having always looked upon it as an event credit-
able to the parties, both of whom are alive and well, or
were a year ago; for it is little more since Evans, now
nigh sixty years old, walked me off my legs on a day's
grousing over Church-mountain, and through Oram's hole,
carrying my kit into the bargain. Adieu. It will be a
long day ere I forget the pool of "Hell-kettle," or the
angels in whose company I first stood by its bubbling
brim.

BEECHER'S RECITATIONS

AND

READINGS.

Humorous, Serious, Dramatic, including Prose and Poetical Selections in Dutch, French, Yankee, Irish, Backwoods, Negro and other Dialects. Edited by Alvah C. Beecher. This excellent selection has been compiled to meet a growing demand for Public Readings, and contains a number of the favorite pieces that have been rendered with telling effect by the most popular Public Readers of the present time. It includes, also, choice selections for Recitations, and is, therefore, admirably adapted for use at Evening Entertainments, School Celebrations, and other Festival occasions.

CONTENTS.

Miss Maloney goes to the Dentist.
Lost and Found. Pathetic.
Mygel Snyder's Barty.
Magdalena ; or, the Spanish Duel.
Jim Wolfe and the Cats.
The Woolen Doll. A Maniac's Story.
The Charity Dinner. A Characteristic Reading.
Go-Morrow ; or, Lot's Wife. Negro Conversation on Religion.
The Wind and the Moon. Recitation.
Dyin' Words of Isaac.
Maude Muller in Dutch.
Moses the Sassy ; or, the Disguised Duke. Burlesque style.
The Yarn of the " Nancy Bell."
Paddy the Piper. Irish Narrative.
Schneider sees " Leah."
Caldwell of Springfield. A Story.
Artemus Ward's Panorama.
Sorrowful Tale of a Servant Girl.
How a Frenchman Entertained John Bull.
Tiamondts on der Prain.
King Robert of Sicily. A Dream.
Gloverson the Mormon.
De Pint wid Ole Pete. Negro Dialect.
Pat and the Pig. An Irish Story.
The Widow Bedott's Letter to Elder Sniffles. Characteristic.
The Cry of the Children.
The Dutchman and the Small-pox.
Sculpin. A Yankee Anecdote.
Rats. Descriptive Recitation.
An Introduction. A Reader Introduces Himself to an Audience.
A Dutchman's Dolly Varden.
" Rock of Ages." A Beautiful Poem.
Feeding the Black Fillies. Irish.
The Hornet. Its Manners and Customs.

The Glove and the Lions.
I Vant to Fly.
That Dog of Jim Smiley's.
The Story of the Faithful Soul.
" My New Pittayatees." Characteristic.
Mary Ann's Wedding.
An Inquiring Yankee.
The Three Bells. Story of a Ship wreck.
Love in a Balloon.
Mrs. Brown on the State of the Streets.
Shoo Flies. " Excelsior " in Dutch.
Discourse by the Rev. Mr. Bosan.
Without the Children. Pathetic.
Signor Billsmethi's Dancing Academy.
Der Goot Lookin Shnow. Parody.
The Celebrated Jumping Frog.
The Lost Chord. A Memory of the Past.
The Tale of a Leg. An Amusing Story.
That West-side Dog.
How Dennis Took the Pledge.
The Fisherman's Summons. Pathetic
Badger's Debut as Hamlet.
How Hezekiah Stole the Spoons.
Paddy's Dream.
Victuals and Drink.
How Jake Schneider Went Blind.
Aurelia's Unfortunate Young Man.
Mrs. Brown on Modern Houses.
Farm Yard Song. Country Scene.
Murphy's Pork Barrel Mystery.
The Prayer Seeker. Pathetic Poem
An Extraordinary Phenomenon.
The Case of Young Bangs.
A Mule Ride in Florida.
Dhree Shkaders. A Dutch Ditty.

Paper covers. Price...**30 cts.**
Bound in boards, cloth back...**50 cts.**

Dick's Original Album Verses and Acrostics.

Containing Original Verses

For Autograph Albums;
To Accompany Bouquets;
For Birthday Anniversaries;
For Wooden, Tin, Crystal, Silver and Golden Weddings;

For Album Dedications;
To Accompany Philopena Forfeits;
For Congratulation;
For Valentines in General, and all Trades and Professions.

It contains also Two Hundred and Eighteen Original Acrostic Verses, the initial letters of each verse forming a different Lady's Christian name, the meaning and derivation of the name being appended to each. The primary object of this book is to furnish entirely fresh and unhackneyed matter for all who may be called upon to fill and adorn a page in a Lady's Album; but it contains also new and appropriate verses to suit Birthday, Wedding, and all other Anniversaries and Occasions to which verses of Compliment or Congratulation are applicable. Paper covers. Price..50 cts.
Bound in full cloth.................................... " ..75 cts.

The Debater, Chairman's Assistant, and Rules of Order. A manual for Instruction and Reference in all matters pertaining to the Management of Public Meetings according to Parliamentary usages. It comprises:

How to Form and Conduct all kinds of Associations and Clubs;
How to Organize and Arrange Public Meetings, Celebrations, Dinners, Picnics and Conventions;
Forms for Constitutions of Lyceums or Institutes, Literary and other Societies;
The Powers and Duties of Officers, with Forms for Treasurers', Secretaries', and other Official Reports;
The Formation and Duties of Committees;

Rules of Order, and Order of Business, with Mode of Procedure in all Cases.
How to draft Resolutions and other Written Business;
A Model Debate, introducing the greatest possible variety of points of order, with correct Decisions by the Chairman;
The Rules of Order, in Tabular Form, for instant reference in all Cases of Doubt that may arise, enabling a Chairman to decide on all points at a glance.

The Work is divided into different Sections, for the purpose of Consecutive Instruction as well as Ready Reference, and includes all Decisions and Rulings up to the present day. Paper covers....................30 cts.
Bound in boards, cloth back................................50 cts.

Dick's Ethiopian Scenes, Variety Sketches and Stump Speeches. Containing End-Men's Jokes,

Negro Interludes and Farces;
Fresh Dialogues for Interlocutor and Banjo;
New Stump Speeches;
Humorous Lectures;

Dialect Sketches and Eccentricities;
Dialogues and Repartee for Interlocutor and Bones;
Quaint Burlesque Sermons;
Jokes, Quips and Gags.

It includes a number of Amusing Scenes and Negro Acts, and is full of the side-splitting vagaries of the best Minstrel Troupes in existence, besides a number of Original Recitations and Sketches in the Negro Dialect. 178 pages, paper covers..30 cts.
Bound in boards, cloth back......................50 cts.

HOWARD'S RECITATIONS.

Comic, Serious and Pathetic. Being a carefully selected collection of fresh Recitations in Prose and Poetry, suitable for Anniversaries, Exhibitions, Social Gatherings, and Evening Parties; affording, also, an abundance of excellent material for practice and declamation. Edited by Clarence J. Howard.

CONTENTS.

Miss Malony on the Chinese Question.
Kit Carson's Ride. A fine descriptive poetical recitation.
Buck Fanshaw's Funeral.
Knocked About. Monologue.
The Puzzled Dutchman. Dialect
Shamus O'Brien. Popular recitation
The Naughty Little Girl. Humorous.
The Bells of Shandon. Serious poem.
No Sect in Heaven. A dream.
Rory O'More's Present to the Priest.
"Mother's Fool." A Recitation.
Queen Elizabeth. A comic oration.
The Starling. A recitation.
Lord Dundreary's Riddle.
The Stuttering Lass. Amusing recital.
The Irish Traveler. Humorous piece.
The Remedy as Bad as the Disease.
A Subject for Dissection.
The Heathen Chinee.
Mona's Waters. Pathetic recitation.
A Showman on the Woodchuck.
How Happy I'll Be. Moral recitation.
A Frenchman's Account of the Fall.
Isabel's Grave. Pathetic recitation.
The Parson and the Spaniel.
An Irishman's Letter.
An Affectionate Letter. Irish style.
The Halibut in Love.
The Merry Soap-Boiler.
The Unbeliever. A solemn recitation
The Voices at the Throne.
Lord Dundreary Proposing. A very comic recitation.
The Fireman. Descriptive piece.
Paul Revere's Ride.
Annie and Willie's Prayer. Pathetic
A Frenchman on Macbeth.
The New Church Organ.
Katrina Likes Me Poody Vell. Humorous Ditty in Dutch dialect.
How to Save a Thousand Pounds.
How I Got Invited to Dinner.
Patient Joe. A serious recitation.
Jimmy Butler and the Owl.
The Menagerie. A wild beast show.
Old Quizzle.
The Infidel and Quaker. Recitation.
The Lawyer and the Chimney-Sweeper.
Bill Mason's Bride. A railroad yarn.
Judging by Appearances.
The Death's Head; or, Honesty the best Policy.
Betsey and I are Out.
Betsey Destroys the Paper.
Father Blake's Collection.
Blank Verse in Rhyme.
Roguery Taught by Confession.
Banty Tim.
Antony and Cleopatra.
Deacon Hezekiah. Description of a Sanctimonious Hypocrite.
The Frenchman and the Landlord.
The Family Quarrel. A dialogue on the Sixteenth Amendment.
The Guess. Old English Recitation.
The Atheist and Acorn.
Brother Watkins Farewell of a Southern Minister.
Hans in a Fix. A Dutchman's dream of Matrimony.
To-Morrow. Poetical recitation.
The Highgate Butcher.
The Lucky Call. The Lost Spectacles.
Challenging the Foreman.
The Country Schoolmaster.
The Matrimonial Bugs and the Travelers.
Peter Sorghum in Love. Yankee story.
Tim Tuff. A sharp bargain.
The Romance of Nick Van Stann.
The Debating Society. Recitation.
Deacon Stokes.
A Tribute to our Honored Dead.
The Dying Soldier. Pathetic poetry.
The Yankee Fireside. Yankee sketches of character.
The Suicidal Cat. An affecting tale.
The Son's Wish. A dying father's bequest.

16mo. 180 pages. Paper covers. Price...............................30 cts.
Bound in boards, cloth back...50 cts.

Dick's Dutch, French and Yankee Dialect

Recitations. An unsurpassed Collection of Droll Dutch Blunders, Frenchmen's Funny Mistakes, and Ludicrous and Extravagant Yankee Yarns, each Recitation being in its own peculiar dialect. To those who make Dialect Recitations a speciality, this Collection will be of particular service, as it contains all the best pieces that are incidentally scattered through a large number of volumes of "Recitations and Readings," besides several new and excellent sketches never before published. 170 pages, paper cover.............................30 cts. Bound in boards, cloth back.......................50 cts.

Dick's Irish Dialect Recitations. A carefully

compiled Collection of Rare Irish Stories, Comic, Poetical and Prose Recitations, Humorous Letters and Funny Recitals, all told with the irresistible Humor of the Irish Dialect. This Collection contains, in addition to new and original pieces, all the very best Recitations in the Irish Dialect that can be gathered from a whole library of "Recitation" books. It is full of the sparkling witticisms and queer conceits of the wittiest nation on earth; and, apart from its special object, it furnishes a fund of the most entertaining matter for perusal in leisure moments. 170 pages, paper cover.............................30 cts. Bound in boards, cloth back.......................50 cts.

Worcester's Letter-Writer and Book of Business Forms for Ladies and Gentlemen. Containing Accu-

rate Directions for Conducting Epistolary Correspondence, with 270 Specimen Letters, adapted to every Age and Situation in Life, and to Business Pursuits in General; with an Appendix comprising Forms for Wills, Petitions, Bills, Receipts, Drafts, Bills of Exchange, Promissory Notes, Executors' and Administrators' Accounts, etc., etc. This work is divided into two parts, the portion applicable to Ladies being kept distinct from the rest of the book, in order to provide better facilities for ready reference. The Orthography of the entire work is based on Worcester's method, which is coming more and more into general use, from the fact that it presents less ambiguity in spelling. 216 pages. Bound in boards, cloth back....50 cts.

SPENCER'S BOOK OF COMIC SPEECHES
AND
HUMOROUS RECITATIONS.

A collection of Comic Speeches and Dialogues, Humorous Prose and Poetical Recitations, Laughable Dramatic Scenes and Burlesques, and Eccentric Characteristic Soliloquies and Stories. Suitable for School Exhibitions and Evening Entertainments. Edited by Albert J. Spencer.

CONTENTS.

Paper covers. Price...**30 cts.**
Bound in boards, cloth back................. ....**50 cts.**

CHECKERS AND CHESS.

Spayth's American Draught Player; or, The Theory and Practice of the Scientific Game of Checkers. Simplified and Illustrated with Practical Diagrams. Containing upwards of 1,700 Games and Positions. By Henry Spayth. Sixth edition, with over three hundred Corrections and Improvements. Containing: The Standard Laws of the Game—Full instructions—Draught Board Numbered—Names of the Games, and how formed—The "Theory of the Move and its Changes" practically explained and illustrated with Diagrams—Playing Tables for Draught Clubs—New Systems of numbering the Board—Prefixing signs to the Variations—List of Draught Treatises and Publications chronologically arranged. Bound in cloth, gilt side and back...$3.00

Spayth's Game of Draughts. By Henry Spayth. This book is designed as a supplement to the author's first work, "The American Draught Player"; but it is complete in itself. It contains lucid instructions for beginners, laws of the game, diagrams, the score of 3:4 games, together with 34 novel, instructive and ingenious "critical positions." Cloth, gilt back and side...$1.50

Spayth's Draughts or Checkers for Beginners. This treatise was written by Henry Spayth, the celebrated player, and is by far the most complete and instructive elementary work on Draughts ever published. It is profusely illustrated with diagrams of ingenious stratagems, curious positions and perplexing problems, and contains a great variety of interesting and instructive Games, progressively arranged and clearly explained with notes, so that the learner may easily comprehend them. With the aid of this Manual a beginner may soon become a proficient in the game. Cloth, gilt side...75 cts.

Scattergood's Game of Draughts, or Checkers, Simplified and Explained. With practical Diagrams and Illustrations, together with a Checker-Board, numbered and printed in red. Containing the Eighteen Standard Games, with over 200 of the best variations, selected from various authors, with some never before published. By D. Scattergood. Bound in cloth, with flexible covers...50 cts.

Marache's Manual of Chess. Containing a description of the Board and Pieces, Chess Notation, Technical Terms, with diagrams illustrating them, Laws of the Game, Relative Value of Pieces. Preliminary Games for Beginners, Fifty Openings of Games, giving all the latest discoveries of Modern Masters, with the best games and copious notes. Twenty Endings of Games, showing easiest ways of effecting Checkmate, Thirty-six ingenious Diagram Problems, and sixteen curious Chess Stratagems, being one of the best Books for Beginners ever published. By N. Marache. Bound in boards, cloth back...50 cts. Bound in cloth, gilt side...75 cts.

DICK & FITZGERALD, Publishers,

Box 2975.   NEW YORK.

READINGS AND RECITATIONS.

Kavanaugh's Juvenile Speaker. For very Little Boys and Girls. Containing short and easily-learned Speeches and Dialogues, expressly adapted for School Celebrations, May-Day Festivals and other Children's Entertainments. Embracing one hundred and twenty-three effective pieces. By Mrs. Russell Kavanaugh. Illuminated paper cover..30 cts. Bound in boards, cloth back..50 cts.

Dick's Series of Recitations and Readings, Nos. 1 to 7. Comprising a carefully compiled selection of Humorous, Pathetic, Eloquent, Patriotic and Sentimental Pieces in Poetry and Prose, exclusively designed for Recitation or Reading. Edited by Wm. B. Dick. Each number of the Series contains about 180 pages. Illud in ed paper cover, each....30 cts. Bound in full cloth...50 cts.

Beecher's Recitations and Readings. Humorous, Serious, Dramatic, including Prose and Poetical Selections in Dutch, Yankee, Irish, Negro and other Dialects. 180 pages, paper covers........ ....30 cts. Bound in boards, cloth back..50 cts.

Howard's Recitations. Comic, Serious and Pathetic. Being a collection of fresh Recitations in Prose and Poetry, suitable for Exhibitions and Evening Parties. 180 pages, paper covers...............30 cts. Bound in boards, cloth back..50 cts.

Spencer's Book of Comic Speeches and Humorous Recitations. A collection of Comic Speeches, Humorous Prose and Poetical Recitations, Laughable Dramatic Scenes and Eccentric Dialect Stories. 192 pages, paper covers...30 cts. Bound in boards, cloth back..50 cts.

Wilson's Book of Recitations and Dialogues. Containing a choice selection of Poetical and Prose Recitations. Designed as an Assistant to Teachers and Students in preparing Exhibitions. 188 pages, paper covers ....30 cts. Bound in boards, with cloth back......................................50 cts.

Barton's Comic Recitations and Humorous Dialogues. A variety of Comic Recitations in Prose and Poetry, Eccentric Orations and Laughable Interludes. 180 pages, paper covers..... ....30 cts. Bound in boards, with cloth back......................................50 cts.

Brudder Bones' Book of Stump Speeches and Burlesque Orations. Also containing Humorous Lectures, Ethiopian Dialogues, Plantation Scenes, Negro Farces and Burlesques, Laughable Interludes and Comic Recitations. 188 pages, paper covers.......................30 cts. Bound in boards, illuminated...50 cts.

Martine's Droll Dialogues and Laughable Recitations. A collection of Humorous Dialogues, Comic Recitations, Brilliant Burlesques and Spirited Stump Speeches. 188 pages, paper covers............30 cts. Bound in boards, with cloth back......................................50 cts.

WE WILL SEND A CATALOGUE containing a complete list of all the pieces in each of the above books, to any person who will send us their address. Send for one.

DICK & FITZGERALD, Publishers,

Box 2975.   **NEW YORK.**

DIALOGUE BOOKS.

The Dialogues contained in these books are all entirely original; some of them being arranged for one sex only, and others for both sexes combined. They develop in a marked degree the eccentricities and peculiarities of the various characters which are represented in them; and are specially adapted for School Exhibitions and other celebrations, which mainly depend upon the efforts of the young folks.

McBride's Comic Dialogues. A collection of twenty-three Original Humorous Dialogues, especially designed for the display of Amateur dramatic talent, and introducing a variety of sentimental, sprightly, comic and genuine Yankee characters, and other ingeniously developed eccentricities. By H. Elliott McBride. 180 pages, illuminated paper covers..30 cts. Bound in boards... ....50 cts.

McBride's All Kinds of Dialogues. A collection of twenty-five Original, Humorous and Domestic Dialogues, introducing Yankee, Irish, Dutch and other characters. Excellently adapted for Amateur Performances. 180 pages, illuminated paper covers....................30 cts. Bound in boards..50 cts.

Holmes' Very Little Dialogues for Very Little Folks. Containing forty-seven New and Original Dialogues, with short and easy parts, almost entirely in words of one syllable, suited to the capacity and comprehension of very young children. Paper covers....................30 cts. Bound in boards, cloth back..50 cts.

Frost's Dialogues for Young Folks. A collection of thirty-six Original, Moral and Humorous Dialogues. Adapted for boys and girls between the ages of ten and fourteen years. By S. A. Frost. 176 pages, paper covers...30 cts. Bound in boards.......................... ....50 cts.

Frost's New Book of Dialogues. Containing twenty-nine entirely New and Original Humorous Dialogues for boys and girls between the ages of twelve and fifteen years. 180 pages, paper covers..........30 cts. Bound in boards, cloth back............. ....50 cts.

Frost's Humorous and Exhibition Dialogues. This is a collection of twenty-five Sprightly Original Dialogues, in Prose and Verse, intended to be spoken at School Exhibitions. 178 pages, paper covers.30 cts. Bound in boards...50 cts.

WE WILL SEND A CATALOGUE free to any address, containing a list of all the Dialogues in each of the above books, together with the number of boys and girls required to perform them.

DICK & FITZGERALD, Publishers,

Box 2975.   NEW YORK.

AMATEUR THEATRICALS.

All the plays in the following excellent books are especially designed for Amateur performance. The majority of them are in one act and one scene, and may be represented in any moderate-sized parlor, without much preparation of costume or scenery.

Burton's Amateur Actor. A complete guide to Private Theatricals; giving plain directions for arranging, decorating and lighting the Stage; with rules and suggestions for mounting, rehearsing and performing all kinds of Plays, Parlor Pantomimes and Shadow Pantomimes. Illustrated with numerous engravings, and including a selection of original Plays, with Prologues, Epilogues, etc. 16mo, illuminated paper cover.....30 cts. Bound in boards, with cloth back.............................50 cts.

Parlor Theatricals; or, Winter Evenings' Entertainment. Containing Acting Proverbs, Dramatic Charades, Drawing-Room Pantomimes, a Musical Burlesque and an amusing Farce, with instructions for Amateurs. Illustrated with engravings. Paper covers...........30 cts. Bound in boards, cloth back....... .. ..50 cts.

Howard's Book of Drawing-Room Theatricals. A collection of twelve short and amusing plays. Some of the plays are adapted for performers of one sex only. 186 pages, paper covers..............30 cts. Bound in boards, with cloth back.. ....50 cts.

Hudson's Private Theatricals. A collection of fourteen humorous plays. Four of these plays are adapted for performance by males only, and three are for females. 180 pages, paper covers.................30 cts Bound in boards, with cloth back......................50 cts.

Nugent's Burlesque and Musical Acting Charades. Containing ten Charades, all in different styles, two of which are easy and effective Comic Parlor Operas, with Music and Piano-forte Accompaniments. 176 pages, paper covers...........................30 cts. Bound in boards, cloth back....................................50 cts.

Frost's Dramatic Proverbs and Charades. Containing eleven Proverbs and fifteen Charades, some of which are for Dramatic Performance, and others arranged for Tableaux Vivants. 176 pages, paper covers.30 cts. Bound in boards, with cloth back............. ....50 cts.

Frost's Parlor Acting Charades. These twelve excellent and original Charades are arranged as short parlor Comedies and Farces, full of brilliant repartee and amusing situations. 182 pages, paper covers..30 cts. Illuminated boards..................... ....50 cts.

Frost's Book of Tableaux and Shadow Pantomimes. A collection of Tableaux Vivants and Shadow Pantomimes, with stage instructions for Costuming, Grouping, etc. 180 pages, paper covers..30 cts. Bound in boards, with cloth back.................................50 cts.

Frost's Amateur Theatricals. A collection of eight original plays; all short, amusing and new. 180 pages, paper covers......30 cts. Bound in boards, with cloth back.............................50 cts.

WE WILL SEND A CATALOGUE containing a complete list of all the pieces in each of the above books, together with the number of male and female characters in each play, to any person who will send us their address. Send for one.

DICK & FITZGERALD, Publishers,
Box 2975.   **NEW YORK.**

Mrs. Partington's Carpet-Bag of Fun.
A collection of over 1,000 of the most Comical Stories, Amusing Adventures, Side-Splitting Jokes, Cheek-extending Poetry, Funny Conundrums, Queer Sayings of Mrs. Partington, Heart-Rending Puns, Witty Repartees, etc. The whole illustrated by about 150 comic wood-cuts. 12mo, 300 pages, ornamented paper covers......................75 cts.

Harp of a Thousand Strings; or, Laughter for a Life-time.
A book of nearly 400 pages; bound in a handsome gilt cover; crowded full of funny stories, besides being illustrated with over 200 comic engravings, by Darley, McLennan, Bellew, etc............ ....$1.50

Chips from Uncle Sam's Jack-Knife.
Illustrated with over 100 Comical Engravings, and comprising a collection of over 500 Laughable Stories, Funny Adventures, Comic Poetry, Queer Conundrums, Terrific Puns and Sentimental Sentences. Large octavo..................35 cts.

Fox's Ethiopian Comicalities.
Containing Strange Sayings, Eccentric Doings, Burlesque Speeches, Laughable Drolleries and Funny Stories, as recited by the celebrated Ethiopian Comedian............10 cts.

Ned Turner's Circus Joke Book.
A collection of the best Jokes, Bon Mots, Repartees, Gems of Wit and Funny Sayings and Doings of the celebrated Equestrian Clown and Ethiopian Comedian, Ned Turner...10 cts.

Ned Turner's Black Jokes.
A collection of Funny Stories, Jokes and Conundrums, interspersed with Witty Sayings and Humorous Dialogues, as given by Ned Turner, the celebrated Ethiopian Delineator...10 cts.

Ned Turner's Clown Joke Book.
Containing the best Jokes and Gems of Wit, composed and delivered by the favorite Equestrian Clown, Ned Turner. Selected and arranged by G. E. G...................10 cts.

Charley White's Joke Book.
Containing a full exposé of all the most laughable Jokes, Witticisms, etc., as told by the celebrated Ethiopian Comedian, Charles White...............................10 cts.

Black Wit and Darky Conversations.
By Charles White. Containing a large collection of laughable Anecdotes, Jokes, Stories, Witticisms and Darky Conversations....................................10 cts.

Yale College Scrapes; or, How the Boys Go It at New Haven.
This is a book of 114 pages, containing accounts of all the famous "Scrapes" and "Sprees" of which students of Old Yale have been guilty for the last quarter of a century ....25 cts.

Laughing Gas.
An Encyclopedia of Wit, Wisdom and Wind. By Sam Slick, Jr. Comically illustrated with 100 original and laughable Engravings, and nearly 500 side-extending Jokes................ 30 cts.

The Knapsack Full of Fun; or, 1,000 Rations of Laughter.
Illustrated with over 100 comical engravings, and containing Jokes and Funny Stories. By Doesticks and other witty writers. Large quarto..30 cts.

The Comical Adventures of David Dufficks.
Illustrated with over one hundred Funny Engravings. This is a book full of fun....25 cts.

The Plate of Chowder.
A Dish for Funny Fellows. Appropriately illustrated with 100 comic engravings. 12mo, paper covers.. 25 cts.

The Young Debater and Chairman's Assistant. By an ex-Member of the Philadelphia Bar. Containing instructions how to Form and Conduct Societies; how to Form and Conduct Clubs and other organized Associations; Rules of Order for the Government of their Business and Debates; how to Compose Resolutions, Reports and Petitions; how to Organize and Manage Public Meetings, Celebrations, Dinners, Pic-Nics and Conventions; Duties of the President and other Officers of a Club or Society, with Official Forms; Hints on Debate and Public Speaking; Forms for Constitutions and By-Laws. To any one who desires to become familiar with the duties of an Officer or Committee-man in a Society or Association this work will be invaluable, as it contains the most minute instructions in everything that pertains to the routine of Society Business.
152 pages, paper covers...30 cts.
Bound in boards, with cloth back......... ....50 cts.

How to Conduct a Debate. A Series of Complete Debates, Outlines of Debates and Questions for Discussion. In the complete debates, the questions for discussion are defined, the debate formally opened, an array of brilliant arguments adduced on either side, and the debate closed according to parliamentary usages. The second part consists of questions for debate, with heads of arguments, for and against, given in a condensed form, for the speakers to enlarge upon to suit their own fancy. In addition to these are a large collection of debatable questions. The authorities to be referred to for information being given at the close of every debate throughout the work. By Frederic Rowton. 232 pages, 16mo.
Paper covers.. ....50 cts.
Bound in boards, cloth back.......................................75 cts.

The Vegetable Garden. Containing thorough instructions for Sowing, Planting and Cultivating all kinds of Vegetables, with plain directions for preparing, manuring and tilling the soil to suit each plant; including, also, a summary of the work to be done in a Vegetable Garden during each month of the year. This work embraces, in a condensed but thoroughly practical form, all the information that either an amateur or a practical gardener can require in connection with the successful raising of Vegetables and Herbs. It also gives separate directions for the cultivation of some seventy different Vegetables, including all the varieties of esculents that form the ordinary stock of a kitchen garden or truck farm. By James Hogg.
140 pages, paper covers.................................. ....30 cts.
Full cloth...50 cts.

The Amateur Trapper and Trap-Maker's Guide. A complete and carefully prepared treatise on the art of Trapping, Snaring and Netting. This comprehensive work is embellished with fifty engraved illustrations; and these, together with the clear explanations which accompany them, will enable anybody of moderate comprehension to make and set any of the traps described. It also gives the baits usually employed by the most successful Hunters and Trappers, and exposes their secret methods of attracting and catching animals, birds, etc., with scarcely a possibility of failure. Large 16mo, paper covers.... ....50 cts.
Bound in boards, cloth back.......................................75 cts.

How to Write a Composition. The use of this excellent handbook will save the student the many hours of labor too often wasted in trying to write a plain composition. It affords a perfect skeleton of one hundred and seventeen different subjects, with their headings or divisions clearly defined, and each heading filled in with the ideas which the subject suggests; so that all the writer has to do, in order to produce a good composition, is to enlarge on them to suit his taste and inclination.
178 pages, paper covers...30 cts.
Bound in boards, cloth back..50 cts.

Barber's American Book of Ready-Made Speeches.
Containing 159 original examples of Humorous and Serious Speeches, suitable for every possible occasion where a speech may be called for, together with appropriate replies to each. Including:

Presentation Speeches.
Convivial Speeches.
Festival Speeches.
Addresses of Congratulation.
Addresses of Welcome.
Addresses of Compliment.
Political Speeches.
Dinner and Supper Speeches for Clubs, etc.

Off-Hand Speeches on a Variety of Subjects.
Miscellaneous Speeches.
Toasts and Sentiments for Public and Private Entertainments.
Preambles and Resolutions of Congratulation, Compliment and Condolence.

With this book any person may prepare himself to make a neat little speech, or reply to one when called upon to do so. They are all short, appropriate and witty, and even ready speakers may profit by them. Paper ....5J cts.
Bound in boards, cloth back..................................... ....75 cts.

Day's American Ready-Reckoner.
By B. H. Day. This Ready-Reckoner is composed of Original Tables, which are positively correct, having been revised in the most careful manner. It is a book of 192 pages, and embraces more matter than 5.0 pages of any other Reckoner. It contains: Tables for Rapid Calculations of Aggregate Values, Wages, Salaries, Board, Interest Money, etc.; Tables of Timber and Plank Measurement; Tables of Board and Log Measurement, and a great variety of Tables and useful calculations which it would be impossible to enumerate in an advertisement of this limited space. All the information in this valuable book is given in a simple manner, and is made so plain, that any person can use it at once without any previous study or loss of time.
Bound in boards, with cloth back....... ....50 cts.
Bound in cloth, gilt back............... ... .75 cts.

The Art and Etiquette of Making Love.
A Manual of Love, Courtship and Matrimony. It tells

How to cure bashfulness,
How to commence a courtship,
How to please a sweetheart or lover,
How to write a love-letter,
How to "pop the question."
How to act before and after a proposal,
How to accept or reject a proposal,

How to break off an engagement,
How to act after an engagement,
How to act as bridesmaid or grooms-man.
How the etiquette of a wedding and the after reception should be observed,

And, in fact, how to fulfill every duty and meet every contingency connected with courtship and matrimony. 175 pages. Paper covers ....30 cts.
Bound in boards, cloth back......................................50 cts.

Frank Converse's Complete Banjo Instructor Without a Master.
Containing a choice collection of Banjo Solos and Hornpipes, Walk Arounds, Reels and Jigs, Songs and Banjo Stories, progressively arranged and plainly explained, enabling the learner to become a proficient banjoist without the aid of a teacher. The necessary explanations accompany each tune, and are placed under the notes on each page, plainly showing the string required, the finger to be used for stopping it, the manner of striking, and the number of times it must be sounded. The Instructor is illustrated with diagrams and explanatory symbols. 100 pages. Bound in boards, cloth back.............................. ....50 cts.

Hard Words Made Easy.
Rules for Pronunciation and Accent; with instructions how to pronounce French, Italian, German, Spanish, and other foreign names....... ....12 cts.

Rarey & Knowlson's Complete Horse Tamer and Farrier.

A New and Improved Edition, containing: Mr. Rarey's Whole Secret of Subduing and Breaking Vicious Horses; His Improved Plan of Managing Young Colts, and Breaking them to the Saddle, to Harness and the Sulky. Rules for Selecting a Good Horse, and for Feeding Horses. Also the Complete Farrier or Horse Doctor; being the result of fifty years' extensive practice of the author, John C. Knowlson, during his life an English Farrier of high popularity; containing the latest discoveries in the cure of Spavin. Illustrated with descriptive engravings. Bound in boards, cloth back. 50 cts.

How to Amuse an Evening Party. A Complete collection of

Home Recreations. Profusely Illustrated with over Two Hundred fine wood-cuts, containing Round Games and Forfeit Games. Parlor Magic and Curious Puzzles, Comic Diversions and Parlor Tricks, Scientific Recreations and Evening Amusements. A young man with this volume may render himself the beau ideal of a delightful companion at every party, and win the hearts of all the ladies, by his powers of entertainment. Bound in ornamental paper covers... 30 cts.
Bound in boards, with cloth back................................50 cts.

Frost's Laws and By-Laws of American Society. A Com-

plete Treatise on Etiquette. Containing plain and Reliable Directions for Deportment in every Situation in Life, by S. A. Frost, author of "Frost's Letter-Writer," etc. This is a book of ready reference on the usages of Society at all times and on all occasions, and also a reliable guide in the details of deportment and polite behavior. Paper covers... ....30 cts.
Bound in boards, with cloth back..............................50 cts.

Frost's Original Letter-Writer. A complete collection of Orig-

inal Letters and Notes, upon every imaginable subject of Every-Day Life, with plain directions about everything connected with writing a letter. By S. A. Frost. To which is added a comprehensive Table of Synonyms, alone worth double the price asked for the book. We assure our readers that it is the best collection of letters ever published in this country; they are written in plain and natural language, and elegant in style without being high-flown. Bound in boards, cloth back, with illuminated sides.................30 cts.

North's Book of Love-Letters. With directions how to write

and when to use them, and 120 Specimen Letters, suitable for Lovers of any age and condition, and under all circumstances. Interspersed with the author's comments thereon. The whole forming a convenient Hand-book of valuable information and counsel for the use of those who need friendly guidance and advice in matters of Love, Courtship and Marriage. By Ingoldsby North. Bound in boards....... ....50 cts.
Bound in cloth......... ....75 cts.

How to Shine in Society; or, The Science of Conversation.

Containing the principles, laws and general usages of polite society, including easily applied hints and directions for commencing and sustaining an agreeable conversation, and for choosing topics appropriate to the time, place and company, thus affording immense assistance to the bashful and diffident. 16mo. Paper covers.....................................15 cts.

The Poet's Companion. A Dictionary of all Allowable Rhymes

in the English Language. This gives the Perfect, the Imperfect and Allowable Rhymes, and will enable you to ascertain to a certainty whether any word can be mated. It is invaluable to any one who desires to court the Muses, and is used by some of the best writers in the country.......25 cts.

Mind Your Stops. Punctuation made plain, and Composition

simplified for Readers, Writers and Talkers.....................12 cts.

Five Hundred French Phrases. A book giving all the French

words and maxims in general use in writing the English language...12 cts.

Sut Lovingood. Yarns spun by "A Nat'ral Born Durn'd Fool."
Warped and Wove for Public Wear, by George W. Harris. Illustrated with eight fine full page engravings, from designs by Howard. It would be difficult, we think, to cram a larger amount of pungent humor into 300 pages than will be found in this really funny book. The Preface and Dedication are models of sly simplicity, and the 24 Sketches which follow are among the best specimens of broad burlesque to which the genius of the ludicrous, for which the Southwest is so distinguished, has yet given birth. 12mo, tinted paper, cloth, gilt edges.......................................$1.00

Uncle Josh's Trunkful of Fun. Containing a rich collection of
Comical Stories, Cruel Sells, Side-Splitting Jokes, Humorous Poetry, Quaint Parodies, Burlesque Sermons, | *New Conundrums, Mirth-Provoking Speeches, Curious Puzzles, Amusing Card Tricks, and Astonishing Feats of Parlor-Magic.*

This book is illustrated with nearly 200 funny engravings, and contains, in 64 large octavo double-column pages, at least three times as much reading matter and real fun as any other book of the price.................. 15 cts.

The Strange and Wonderful Adventures of Bachelor Butterly.
Showing how his passion for Natural History completely eradicated the tender passion implanted in his breast—also detailing his Extraordinary Travels, both by sea and land—his Hair-breadth Escapes from fire and cold—his being come over by a Widow with nine small children—his wonderful Adventures with the Doctor and the Fiddler, and other Perils of a most extraordinary nature. The whole illustrated by about 200 engravings..30 cts.

The Laughable Adventures of Messrs. Brown, Jones and Robinson.
Showing where they went, and how they went, what they did, and how they did it. Here is a book which will make you split your sides laughing. It shows the comical adventures of three jolly young greenhorns, who went traveling, and got into all manner of scrapes and funny adventures. Illustrated with nearly 200 thrillingly-comic engravings.....30 cts.

The Mishaps and Adventures of Obadiah Oldbuck.
This humorous and curious book sets forth, with 188 comic drawings, the misfortunes which befell Mr. Oldbuck; and also his five unsuccessful attempts to commit suicide—his hair-breadth escapes from fire, water and famine—his affection for his poor dog, etc. To look over this book will make you laugh, and you can't help it...................................20 cts.

Jack Johnson's Jokes for the Jolly.
A collection of Funny Stories, Droll Incidents, Queer Conceits and Apt Repartees. Illustrating the Drolleries of Border Life in the West, Yankee Peculiarities, Dutch Blunders, French Sarcasms, Irish Wit and Humor, etc., with short Ludicrous Narratives; making altogether a Medley of Mirthful Morsels for the Melancholy that will drive away the blues, and cause the most misanthropic mortal to laugh. Illustrated paper covers......................25 cts.

Snipsnaps and Snickerings of Simon Snodgrass.
A collection of Droll and Laughable Stories, illustrative of Irish Drolleries and Blarney, Ludicrous Dutch Blunders, Queer Yankee Tricks and Dodges, Backwoods Boasting, Humors of Horse-trading, Negro Comicalities, Perilous Pranks of Fighting Men, Frenchmen's Queer Mistakes, Scotch Shrewdness, and other phases of eccentric character, that go to make up a perfect and complete Medley of Wit and Humor. It is also full of funny engravings..25 cts.

Madame Le Normand's Fortune Teller. An entertaining book, said to have been written by Madame Le Normand, the celebrated French Fortune Teller, who was frequently consulted by the Emperor Napoleon. A party of ladies and gentlemen may amuse themselves for hours with this curious book. It tells fortunes by "The Chart of Fate" (a large lithographic chart), and gives 624 answers to questions on every imaginable subject that may happen in the future. It explains a variety of ways for telling fortunes by Cards and Dice; gives a list of 79 curious old superstitions and omens, and 187 weather omens, and winds up with the celebrated Oraculum of Napoleon. We will not endorse this book as infallible; but we assure our readers that it is the source of much mirth whenever introduced at a gathering of ladies and gentlemen. Bound in boards. **40 cts.**

The Fireside Magician; or, The Art of Natural Magic
Made Easy. Being a scientific explanation of Legerdemain, Physical Amusement, Recreative Chemistry, Diversion with Cards, and of all the mysteries of Mechanical Magic, with feats as performed by Herr Alexander, Robert Heller, Robert Houdin, "The Wizard of the North," and distinguished conjurors—comprising two hundred and fifty interesting mental and physical recreations, with explanatory engravings. 132 pages, paper. **30 cts.**
Bound in boards, cloth back...**50 cts.**

Howard's Book of Conundrums and Riddles. Containing
over 1,200 of the best Conundrums, Riddles, Enigmas, Ingenious Catches and Amusing Sells ever invented. This splendid collection of curious paradoxes will afford the material for a never-ending feast of fun and amusement. Any person, with the assistance of this book, may take the lead in entertaining a company, and keep them in roars of laughter for hours together.
Paper covers ....**30 cts.**
Bound in boards, cloth back...**50 cts.**

The Parlor Magician; or, One Hundred Tricks for the
Drawing-Room. Containing an extensive and miscellaneous collection of Conjuring and Legerdemain, embracing: Tricks with Dice, Dominoes and Cards; Tricks with Ribbons, Rings and Fruit; Tricks with Coin, Handkerchiefs and Balls, etc. The whole illustrated and clearly explained with 121 engravings. Paper covers...**30 cts.**
Bound in boards, with cloth back...**50 cts.**

Book of Riddles and 500 Home Amusements. Containing
a curious collection of Riddles, Charades and Enigmas; Rebuses, Anagrams and Transpositions; Conundrums and Amusing Puzzles; Recreations in Arithmetic, and Queer Sleights, and numerous other Entertaining Amusements. Illustrated with 60 engravings. Paper covers..............**30 cts.**
Bound in boards, with cloth back...**50 cts.**

The Book of Fireside Games. Containing an explanation of a
variety of Witty, Rollicking, Entertaining and Innocent Games and Amusing Forfeits, suited to the Family Circle as a Recreation. This book is just the thing for social gatherings, parties and pic-nics. Paper covers .**30 cts.**
Bound in boards, cloth back...**50 cts.**

The Book of 500 Curious Puzzles. Containing a large collec-
tion of Curious Puzzles, Entertaining Paradoxes, Perplexing Deceptions in Numbers, Amusing Tricks in Geometry; illustrated with a great variety of Engravings. Paper covers...**30 cts.**
Bound in boards, with cloth back...**50 cts.**

Parlor Tricks with Cards. Containing explanations of all the
Tricks and Deceptions with Playing Cards ever invented. The whole illustrated and made plain and easy with 70 engravings. Paper covers..**30 cts.**
Bound in boards, with cloth back...**50 cts.**

Day's Book-Keeping Without a Master.

Containing the Rudiments of Book-keeping in Single and Double Entry, together with the proper Forms and Rules for opening and keeping condensed and general Book Accounts. This work is printed in a beautiful script type, and hence combines the advantages of a handsome style of writing with its very simple and easily understood lessons in Book-keeping. The several pages have explanations at the bottom to assist the learner, in small type. As a pattern for opening book accounts it is especially valuable—particularly for those who are not well posted in the art. DAY'S BOOK-KEEPING is the size of a regular quarto Account Book, and is made to lie flat open for convenience in use...50 cts.

Blank Books for Day's Book-Keeping.

We have for sale Books of 96 pages each, ruled according to the patterns mentioned on page 3 of DAY'S BOOK-KEEPING, suitable for practice of the learner, viz.: No. 1—For General Book-keeping, pages 4 and 5; for Cash Account on page 13; for Day-Book in Single Entry, pages 15 to 25. No. 2—For Condensed Accounts, pages 9 and 10; for Cash Account, page 12; for Journal in Double Entry, pages 34 to 43. No. 3—For Ledgers in Double or Single Entry, pages 26 to 44. Each Number ....50 cts.

How to Learn the Sense of 3,000 French Words in one

Hour. This ingenious little book actually accomplishes all that its title claims. It is a fact that there are at least three thousand words in the French language, forming a large proportion of those used in ordinary conversation, which are spelled exactly the same as in English, or become the same by very slight and easily understood changes in their termination. 16mo, illuminated paper covers...25 cts.

How to Speak in Public; or, The Art of Extempore Oratory.

A valuable manual for those who desire to become ready off-hand speakers; containing clear directions how to arrange ideas logically and quickly, including illustrations, by the analysis of speeches delivered by some of the greatest orators, exemplifying the importance of correct emphasis, clearness of articulation, and appropriate gesture. Paper covers..............25 cts.

Live and Learn.

A guide for all those who wish to speak and write correctly; particularly intended as a Book of Reference for the solution of difficulties connected with Grammar, Composition, Punctuation, &c., &c., containing examples of 1,000 mistakes of daily occurrence in speaking, writing and pronunciation. Cloth, 16mo, 216 pages..............75 cts.

The Art of Dressing Well.

By Miss S. A. Frost. This book is designed for ladies and gentlemen who desire to make a favorable impression upon society. Paper covers.......................................30 cts.
Bound in boards, cloth back..50 cts.

Thimm's French Self-Taught.

A new system, on the most simple principles, for Universal Self-Tuition, with English pronunciation of every word. By this system the acquirement of the French Language is rendered less laborious and more thorough than by any of the old methods. By Franz Thimm ....25 cts.

Thimm's German Self-Taught.

Uniform with "French Self-Taught," and arranged in accordance with the same principles of thoroughness and simplicity. By Franz Thimm..............................25 cts.

Thimm's Spanish Self-Taught.

A book of self-instruction in the Spanish Language, arranged according to the same method as the "French" and "German," by the same author, and uniform with them in size. By Franz Thimm...25 cts.

Thimm's Italian Self-Taught.

Uniform in style and size with the three foregoing books. By Franz Thimm........................25 cts.

CARD AND OTHER GAMES.

"Trump's" American Hoyle; or, Gentleman's Hand-Book of Games. This work contains an exhaustive treatise on Whist, by William Pole, F.R.S., and the rules for playing that game as laid down by the Hon. James Clay. It also contains clear descriptions of all the games played in the United States, with the American rules for playing them; including Euchre, Bézique, Cribbage, All Fours, Loo, Poker, Brag, Piquet, Pedro Sancho, Penuchle, Railroad Euchre, Jack Pots. Ecarté, Boston, Cassino, Chess, Checkers, Backgammon, Billiards, Dominoes, and a hundred other games. This work is designed as an American authority in all games of skill and chance, and will settle any disputed point. It has been prepared with great care, and is not a re-hash of English games, but a live American book, expressly prepared for American players. THE AMERICAN HOYLE contains 525 pages, is printed on fine white paper, bound in cloth, with extra gilt side and beveled boards, and is profusely illustrated.............$2.00

The Modern Pocket Hoyle. By "Trumps." Containing all the games of skill and chance, as played in this country at the present time, being an "authority on all disputed points." This valuable manual is all original, or thoroughly revised from the best and latest authorities, and includes the laws and complete directions for playing one hundred and eleven different games. 388 pages, paper covers..............50 cts.
Bound in boards, with cloth back.............75 cts.
Bound in cloth, gilt side and back.............$1.25

Hoyle's Games. A complete Manual of the laws that govern all games of skill and chance, including Card Games, Chess, Checkers, Dominoes, Backgammon, Dice, Billiards (as played in this country at the present time), and all Field Games. Entirely original, or thoroughly revised from the latest and best American authorities. Paper covers.............50 cts.
Boards.............75 cts.
Cloth, gilt side.............$1.25

Walker's Cribbage Made Easy. Being a new and complete Treatise on the Game in all varieties. By George Walker, Esq. A very comprehensive work on this Game. It contains over 500 examples of how to discard for your own and your adversary's crib.
142 pages, bound in boards.............50 cts.

100 Tricks With Cards Exposed and Explained. By J. H. Green, the Reformed Gambler. This book exposes and explains all the Mysteries of the Gambling Tables. It is interesting not only to those who play, but to those who do not. Paper covers.............30 cts.
Bound in boards, with cloth back.............50 cts.

How Gamblers Win; or, The Secrets of Advantage Playing Exposed. Being a complete and scientific exposé of the manner of playing all the various advantages in the various Card Games, as practiced by professional gamblers. This work is designed as a warning to self-confident card-players. Bound in boards, with cloth back.............50 cts.

DICK & FITZGERALD, Publishers,

Box 2975.   NEW YORK.

Martine's Sensible Letter-Writer.

Being a comprehensive and complete Guide and Assistant for those who desire to carry on Epistolary Correspondence; containing a large collection of model letters on the simplest matters of life, adapted to all ages and conditions—

EMBRACING,

Business Letters ;	Letters of Courtesy, Friendship and
Applications for Employment, with	Affection ;
Letters of Recommendation and	Letters of Condolence and Sympathy ;
Answers to Advertisements ;	A Choice Collection of Love-Letters,
Letters between Parents and Children;	for Every Situation in a Courtship ;
Letters of Friendly Counsel and Re-	Notes of Ceremony. Familiar Invita-
monstrance ;	tions, etc., together with Notes of
Letters soliciting Advice, Assistance	Acceptance and Regret.
and Friendly Favors ;	

The whole containing 300 Sensible Letters and Notes. This is an invaluable book for those persons who have not had sufficient practice to enable them to write letters without great effort. It contains such a variety of letters, that models may be found to suit every subject.

257 pages, bound in boards, cloth back............................50 cts.
Bound in cloth..75 cts.

Martine's Hand-Book of Etiquette and Guide to True

Politeness. A complete Manual for all those who desire to understand good breeding, the customs of good society, and to avoid incorrect and vulgar habits. Containing clear and comprehensive directions for correct manners, conversation, dress, introductions, rules for good behavior at Dinner Parties and the Table, with hints on carving and wine at table; together with the Etiquette of the Ball and Assembly Room, Evening Parties, and the usages to be observed when visiting or receiving calls; Deportment in the street and when traveling. To which is added the Etiquette of Courtship, Marriage, Domestic Duties and fifty-six rules to be observed in general society. By Arthur Martine. Bound in boards ..50 cts.
Bound in cloth, gilt sides..75 cts.

Dick's Quadrille Call-Book and Ball-Room Prompter.

Containing clear directions how to call out the figures of every dance, with the quantity of music necessary for each figure, and simple explanations of all the figures which occur in Plain and Fancy Quadrilles. This book gives plain and comprehensive instructions how to dance all the new and popular dances, fully describing

The Opening March or Polonaise,	March and Cheat Quadrilles,
Various Plain and Fancy Quadrilles,	Favorite Jigs and Contra-Dances,
Waltz and Glide Quadrilles,	Polka and Polka Redowa,
Plain Lancers and Caledonians,	Redowa and Redowa Waltz,
Glide Lancers and Caledonians,	Polka Mazourka and Old Style Waltz,
Saratoga Lancers,	Modern Plain Waltz and Glide,
The Parisian Varieties,	Boston Dip and Hop Waltz,
The Prince Imperial Set.	Five-Step Waltz and Schottische.
Social and Basket Quadrilles,	Varsovienne and Zulma L'Orientale,
Nine-Pin and Star Quadrilles,	Galop and Deux Temps,
Gavotte and Minuet Quadrilles,	Esmeralda, Sicilienne, Danish Dance,

AND OVER ONE HUNDRED FIGURES FOR THE "GERMAN;"

To which is added a Sensible Guide to Etiquette and Proper Deportment in the Ball and Assembly Room, besides seventy pages of dance music for the piano.

Paper covers..50 cts.
Bound in boards..75 cts.

Lola Montez' Arts of Beauty; or, Secrets of a Lady's Toilet.

With hints to Gentlemen on the Art of Fascinating. Lola Montez here explains all the Arts employed by the celebrated beauties and fashionable ladies in Paris and other cities of Europe, for the purpose of preserving their beauty and improving and developing their charms. The recipes are all clearly given, so that any person can understand them, and the work embraces the following subjects:

How to obtain such desirable and indispensable attractions as A Handsome Form ;
A Bright and Smooth Skin ;
A Beautiful Complexion ;
Attractive Eyes, Mouth and Lips ;
A Beautiful Hand, Foot and Ankle ;
A Well-trained Voice ;

A Soft and Abundant Head of Hair; Also, How to Remedy Gray Hair; And harmless but effectual methods of removing Superfluous Hair and other blemishes, with interesting information on these and kindred matters.

Illuminated paper cover..25 cts.

Hillgrove's Ball-Room Guide and Complete Dancing-Master.

Containing a plain treatise on Etiquette and Deportment at Balls and Parties, with valuable hints on Dress and the Toilet, together with

Full Explanations of the Rudiments, Terms, Figures and Steps used in Dancing;
Including Clear and Precise Instructions how to dance all kinds of Quadrilles, Waltzes, Polkas, Redowas,

Reels, Round, Plain and Fancy Dances, so that any person may learn them without the aid of a Teacher;
To which is added easy directions how to call out the Figures

of every dance, and the amount of music required for each. Illustrated with 176 descriptive engravings. By T. Hillgrove, Professor of Dancing.
Bound in cloth, with gilt side and back............................$1.00
Bound in boards, with cloth back.................................75 cts.

The Banjo, and How to Play it.

Containing, in addition to the elementary studies, a choice collection of Polkas, Waltzes, Solos, Schottisches, Songs, Hornpipes, Jigs, Reels, etc., with full explanations of both the "Banjo" and "Guitar" styles of execution, and designed to impart a complete knowledge of the art of playing the Banjo practically, without the aid of a teacher. This work is arranged on the progressive system, showing the learner how to play the first few notes of a tune, then the next notes, and so on, a small portion at a time, until he has mastered the entire piece, every detail being as clearly and thoroughly explained as if he had a teacher at his elbow all the time. By Frank B. Converse, author of the "Banjo without a Master." 16mo, bound in boards, cloth back..50 cts.

Row's National Wages Tables.

Showing at a glance the amount of wages from half an hour to sixty hours, at from $1 to $37 per week. Also from one-quarter of a day to four weeks, at $1 to $37 per week. By Nelson Row. By this book, which is particularly useful when part of a week, day or hour is lost, a large pay-roll can be made out in a few minutes, thus saving more time in making out one pay-roll than the cost of the book. Every employer hiring help by the hour, day or week, and every employee, should obtain one, as it will enable him to know exactly the amount of money he is entitled to on pay-day. Half bound..................50 cts.

Row's Complete Fractional Ready-Reckoner.

For buying and selling any kind of merchandise, giving the fractional parts of a pound, yard, etc., from one-quarter to one thousand, at any price from one-quarter of a cent to five dollars. By Nelson Row. 36mo, 234 pages, boards..50 cts.

Blunders in Behavior Corrected.

A book of Deportment for both Ladies and Gentlemen. By means of this book you can learn the most difficult phases in Etiquette, or behavior in good society............12 cts.

Delisser's Horseman's Guide.
Comprising the Laws on Warranty, and the Rules in purchasing and selling horses, with the decisions and reports of various courts in Europe and the United States; to which is added a detailed account of what constitutes soundness and unsoundness, and a precise method, simply laid down, for the examination of horses, showing their age to thirty years old; together with an exposure of the various tricks and impositions practiced by low horse-dealers (jockeys) on inexperienced persons; also, a valuable Table of each and every bone in the structure of the Horse. By George P. Delisser, Veterinary Surgeon.
Bound in boards, cloth back..75 cts.
Bound in cloth...$1.00

Brisbane's Golden Ready-Reckoner.
Calculated in Dollars and Cents. Showing at once the amount or value of any number of articles or quantity of goods, or any merchandise, either by the gallon, quart, pint, ounce, pound, quarter, hundred, yard, foot, inch, bushel, etc., in an easy and plain manner. To which are added Interest Tables, calculated in dollars and cents, for days and for months, at six per cent. and at seven per cent. per annum, alternately; and a great number of other Tables and Rules for calculation never before in print. Bound in boards.................35 cts.

How to Cook Potatoes, Apples, Eggs and Fish, Four Hundred Different Ways.
Our lady friends will be surprised when they examine this book, and find the great variety of ways that the same article may be prepared and cooked. The work especially recommends itself to those who are often embarrassed for want of variety in dishes suitable for the breakfast-table, or on occasions where the necessity arises for preparing a meal at short notice. Paper covers.............................30 cts.
Bound in boards, with cloth back.............................50 cts.

The American Housewife and Kitchen Directory.
This valuable book embraces three hundred and seventy-eight recipes for cooking all sorts of American dishes in the most economical manner; it also contains a variety of important secrets for washing, cleaning, scouring and extracting grease, paint, stains and iron-mould from cloth, muslin and linen. Bound in ornamental paper covers......... ....30 cts.
Bound in boards, with cloth back.............................50 cts.

How to Cook and How to Carve.
Giving plain and easily understood directions for preparing and cooking, with the greatest economy, every kind of dish, with complete instructions for serving the same. This book is just the thing for a young Housekeeper. It is worth a dozen of expensive French books. Paper covers.............................30 cts.
Bound in boards, with cloth back.............................50 cts.

The American Home Cook Book.
Containing several hundred excellent recipes. The whole based on many years' experience of an American Housewife. Illustrated with engravings. All the Recipes in this book are written from actual experience in Cooking. Paper....30 cts.
Bound in boards, cloth back...................................50 cts.

The Yankee Cook Book.
A new system of Cookery. Containing hundreds of excellent recipes from actual experience in Cooking; also, full explanations in the art of Carving. 126 pages. paper covers.30 cts.
Bound in boards, with cloth back.............................50 cts.

How to Mix all Kinds of Fancy Drinks.
Containing clear and reliable directions for mixing all the beverages used in the United States. Embracing Punches, Juleps, Cobblers, Cocktails, etc., etc., in endless variety. By Jerry Thomas. Illuminated paper covers.....................50 cts.
Bound in full cloth.....................................75 cts.

What Shall We Do To-Night? or, Social Amusements for

Evening Parties. This elegant book affords an almost inexhaustible fund of amusement for evening parties, social gatherings and all festive occasions, ingeniously grouped together so as to furnish complete and ever-varying entertainment for Twenty-six evenings. Its repertoire embraces all the best round and forfeit games, clearly described and rendered perfectly plain by original and amusing examples, interspersed with a great variety of ingenious puzzles, entertaining tricks and innocent sells; new and original Musical and Poetical pastimes, startling illusions and mirth-provoking exhibitions; including complete directions and text for performing Charades, Tableaux, Parlor Pantomimes, the world-renowned Punch and Judy, Gallanty Shows and original Shadow-pantomimes; also, full information for the successful performance of Dramatic Dialogues and Parlor Theatricals, with a selection of Original Plays, etc., written expressly for this work. It is embellished with over one hundred descriptive and explanatory engravings, and contains 366 pages, printed on fine toned paper. Extra cloth...**$2.00**

The Secret Out; or, 1,000 Tricks with Cards, and Other

Recreations. Illustrated with over 300 engravings. A book which explains all the Tricks and Deceptions with Playing Cards ever known, and gives, besides, a great many new ones. The whole being described so carefully, with engravings to illustrate them, that anybody can easily learn how to perform them. This work also contains 240 of the best Tricks of Legerdemain, in addition to the Card Tricks. Such is the unerring process of instruction adopted in this volume, that no reader can fail to succeed in executing every Trick, Experiment, Game, etc., set down, if he will at all devote his attention, in his leisure hours, to the subject; and, as almost every trick with cards known will be found in this collection, it may be considered the only complete work on the subject ever published.
12mo, 400 pages, bound in cloth, gilt side and back...................**$1.50**

The Magician's Own Book; or, The Whole Art of Con-

juring. A complete hand-book of Parlor Magic, containing over a thousand Optical, Chemical, Mechanical, Magnetic and Magical Experiments, Amusing Transmutations, Astonishing Sleights and Subtleties, Celebrated Card Deceptions, Ingenious Tricks with Numbers, curious and entertaining Puzzles, the Art of Secret Writing, together with all the most noted tricks of modern performers. Illustrated with over 500 wood-cuts, the whole forming a comprehensive guide for amateurs. 12mo, cloth, gilt... ..**$1.50**

The Sociable; or, One Thousand and One Home Amuse-

ments. Containing Acting Proverbs, Dramatic Charades, Acting Charades or Drawing-room Pantomimes, Musical Burlesques, Tableaux Vivants, Parlor Games, Games of Action, Forfeits, Science in Sport and Parlor Magic, and a choice collection of curious Mental and Mechanical Puzzles, etc. Illustrated with numerous engravings and diagrams. The whole being a fund of never-ending entertainment. 376 pages, cloth, gilt......**$1.50**

Athletic Sports for Boys. A Repository of Graceful Recrea-

tions for Youth, containing clear and complete instructions in Gymnastics, Limb Exercises, Jumping, Pole-Leaping, Dumb Bells, Indian Clubs, Parallel Bars, the Horizontal Bar, the Trapeze, the Suspended Ropes, and the manly accomplishments of Skating, Swimming, Rowing, Sailing, Horsemanship, Riding, Driving, Angling, Fencing and Broadsword. Illustrated with 194 wood-cuts. Bound in boards................**75 cts.**

The Young Reporter; or, How to Write Short-Hand. A

Complete Phonographic Teacher, intended as a School-book, to afford thorough instructions to those who have not the assistance of an Oral Teacher. By the aid of this work, any person of the most ordinary intelligence may learn to write Short-Hand, and report Speeches and Sermons in a short time. Bound in boards, with cloth back........... ....**50 cts.**

The Biblical Reason Why. A Hand-Book for

Biblical Students, and a guide to family Scripture reading. This work gives REASONS founded upon the Bible, and assigned by the most eminent Divines and Christian Philosophers, for the great and all-absorbing events recorded in the History of the Bible, the Life of our Saviour and the Acts of His Apostles.

EXAMPLE.

Why did the first patriarchs attain such extreme longevity?
Why was the term of life afterwards shortened?
Why are there several manifest variations in names, facts and dates, between the books of Kings and Chronicles?

Why is the book of the Prophecies of Isaiah a strong proof of the authenticity of the whole Bible?
Why did our Saviour receive the name of Jesus?
Why did John the Baptist hesitate to administer the rite of Baptism to Jesus?

This volume answers 1,493 similar questions. Beautifully illustrated. Large 12mo, cloth, gilt side and back..........$1.50

The Reason Why: General Science. A careful collection of reasons for some thousands of things which, though generally known, are imperfectly understood. A book for the million. This work assigns reasons for the thousands of things that daily fall under the eye of the intelligent observer, and of which he seeks a simple and clear explanation.

EXAMPLE.

Why does silver tarnish when exposed to light?
Why do some colors fade, and others darken, when exposed to the sun?
Why is the sky blue?

What develops electricity in the clouds?
Why does dew form round drops upon the leaves of plants?

This volume answers 1,325 similar questions. 356 pages, bound in cloth, gilt, and embellished with a large number of woodcuts, illustrating the various subjects treated of..........$1.50

The Reason Why: Natural History. Giving reasons for hundreds of interesting facts in connection with Zoology, and throwing a light upon the peculiar habits and instincts of the various orders of the Animal Kingdom.

EXAMPLE.

Why has the lion such a large mane?
Why does the otter, when hunting for fish, swim against the stream?
Why do dogs turn around two or three times before they lie down?
Why have flat fishes their upper sides dark, and their under sides white?

Why do sporting dogs make what is termed "a point"?
Why do birds often roost upon one leg?
Why do frogs keep their mouths closed while breathing?
Why does the wren build several nests, but occupy only one?

This volume answers about 1,500 similar questions.
Illustrated, cloth, gilt side and back..................$1.50

The American Boy's Book of Sports and

Games. A Repository of In and Out-door Amusements for Boys and Youths. Containing 600 large 12mo pages. Illustrated with nearly 700 engravings, designed by White, Herrick, Weir and Harvey, and engraved by N. Orr. This is unquestionably the most attractive and valuable book of its kind ever issued in this or any other country. It was three years in preparation, and embraces all the sports and games that tend to develop the physical constitution, improve the mind and heart, and relieve the tedium of leisure hours, both in the parlor and the field.

The engravings are in the first style of the art, and embrace eight full-page ornamental titles, and two large colored chromos, illustrating the several departments of the work, beautifully printed on tinted paper. The book is issued in the best style, being printed on fine sized paper, and handsomely bound. Extra cloth, gilt side and back, extra gold, beveled boards.....**$2.00**

Jack Johnson's Jokes for the Jolly. A collection of Funny Stories, illustrating the Drolleries of Border Life in the West, Yankee Peculiarities, Dutch Blunders, French Sarcasms, Irish Wit and Humor, etc.

Illustrated paper covers...........................**25 cts.**

The Art and Etiquette of Making Love. A

Manual of Love, Courtship and Matrimony. It tells

How to Cure Bashfulness;
How to Commence a Courtship;
How to Please a Sweetheart or Lover;
How to Write a Love-Letter;
How to " Pop the Question";
How to Act Before and After a Proposal;
How to Accept or Reject a Proposal;
How to Break off an Engagement;
How to Act After an Engagement;
How to Act as Bridesmaid or Grooms-man;
How the Etiquette of a Wedding and the After-Reception Should be Observed;

And, in fact, how to fulfill every duty and meet every contingency connected with courtship and matrimony. It includes also a choice collection of sensible Letters suitable for all the contingencies of Love and Courtship.

176 pages, paper covers................................**30 cts.**
Bound in boards, cloth back...... ....**50 cts.**

Dick's Quadrille Call-Book and Ball-Room Prompter.

Containing clear directions how to call out the figures of every dance, with the quantity of music necessary for each figure, and simple explanations of all the figures and steps which occur in Plain and Fancy Quadrilles. Also, a analysis and description of all the steps employed in the favorite round dances, fully describing:

The Opening March or Polonaise,	*March and Cheat Quadrilles,*
Various Plain and Fancy Quadrilles,	*Favorite Jigs and Contra-Dances,*
Waltz and Glide Quadrilles,	*Polka and Polka Redowa,*
Plain Lancers and Caledonians,	*Redowa and Redowa Waltz,*
Glide Lancers and Caledonians,	*Polka Mazourka and Old Style Waltz,*
Saratoga Lancers,	*Modern Plain Waltz and Glide,*
The Parisian Varieties,	*Boston Dip and Hop Waltz,*
The Prince Imperial Set,	*Five-Step Waltz and Scholtische,*
Social and Basket Quadrilles,	*Varsovienne, and Zulma L'Orientale,*
Nine-Pin and Star Quadrilles,	*Galop and Deux Temps,*
Gavotte and Minuet Quadrilles,	*Esmeralda, Sicilienne, Danish Dance,*

AND OVER ONE HUNDRED FIGURES FOR THE "GERMAN;"

To which is added a Sensible Guide to Etiquette and Proper Deportment in the Ball and Assembly Room, besides seventy pages of dance music for the piano.

Paper covers...**50 cts.**
Bound in boards......................................**75 cts.**

Uncle Josh's Trunkful of Fun. A portfolio of

first-class Wit and Humor, and never-ending source of Jollity.

CONTAINING A RICH COLLECTION OF

Comical Stories, Cruel Sells,
Side-Splitting Jokes,
Humorous Poetry,
Quaint Parodies,
Burlesque Sermons,

New Conundrums,
Mirth-Provoking Speeches,
Curious Puzzles,
Amusing Card Tricks, and
Astonishing Feats of Parlor-Magic.

This book is illustrated with nearly 200 Funny Engravings, and
contains 64 large octavo double-column pages... ....**15 cts.**

Barber's American Book of Ready-Made

Speeches. Containing 159 original examples of Humorous and
Serious Speeches, suitable for every possible occasion where a
speech may be called for, with appropriate replies to each.

INCLUDING

Presentation Speeches.
Convivial Speeches.
Festival Speeches.
Addresses of Congratulation.
Addresses of Welcome.
Addresses of Compliment.
Political Speeches.
Dinner and Supper Speeches for
Clubs, etc.

Off-Hand Speeches on a Variety of
Subjects.
Miscellaneous Speeches.
Toasts and Sentiments for Public and
Private Entertainments.
Preambles and Resolutions of Congratulation, Compliment and Condolence.

With this book any person may prepare himself to make a neat
little speech, or reply to one when called upon to do so. They
are all short, appropriate and witty, and even ready speakers
may profit by them. Paper......................**50 cts.**
Bound in boards, cloth back........................**75 cts.**

The Amateur Trapper and Trap-Maker's

Guide. A complete and carefully prepared treatise on the art of Trapping, Snaring and Netting; containing plain directions for constructing the most approved Traps, Snares, Nets and Dead-Falls; the best methods of applying them to their various purposes; and the most successful Baits for attracting all kinds of Animals, Birds, etc., with their special uses in each case; introducing receipts for preparing Skins and Furs for Market.

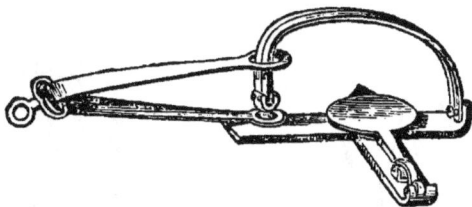

The entire work is based on the experience of the most successful Trappers, and on information derived from other authentic professional sources. By Stanley Harding. This comprehensive work is embellished with fifty well drawn and engraved illustrations; and these, together with the clear explanations which accompany them, will enable anybody of moderate comprehension to make and set any of the traps described. IT TELLS

How to make all kinds of Traps;
How to make all kinds of Snares;
How to Set and Secure Traps;
How to Attract Animals from a Distance;
How to Prepare Baits;
How to Bait a Trap;
How to Trap or Snare all kinds of Animals;
How to Trap or Snare Birds of every description;
How to Cure and Tan Skins;
How to Skin and Stuff Birds or Animals.

It also gives the baits usually employed by the most successful Hunters and Trappers, and exposes their secret methods of attracting and catching Animals, Birds, etc., with scarcely a possibility of failure. Large 16mo, paper covers.........**50 cts.**
Bound in boards, cloth back.......................**75 cts.**

How to Write a Composition. This original

work will be found a valuable aid in writing a composition on any topic. It lays down plain directions for the division of a subject into its appropriate heads, and for arranging them in their natural order, commencing with the simplest theme, and advancing progressively to more complicated subjects. Paper..**30 cts.**
Bound in boards, cloth back........................**50 cts.**

The Magician's Own Book.
One of the most extraordinary and interesting volumes ever printed—containing the Whole Art of Conjuring, and all the Discoveries in Magic ever made, either by ancient or modern philosophers. IT EXPLAINS

All Sleight of Hand Tricks;
Tricks and Deceptions with Cards;
The Magic of Chemistry;
Mysterious Experiments in Electricity and Galvanism;
The Magic of Pneumatics, Acrostatics, Optics, etc.;
The Magic of Numbers;

Curious Tricks in Geometry;
Mysterious and Amusing Puzzles, and answers thereto;
The Magic of Art;
Miscellaneous Tricks and Experiments;
Curious Fancies, etc., etc.

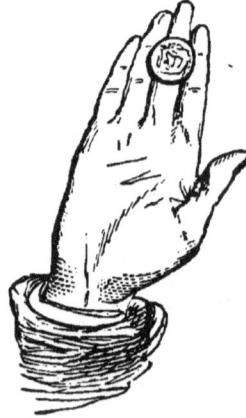

The tricks are all illustrated by Engravings and Tables, so as to make them easily understood and practiced. As a volume for the amusement of an evening party, this book cannot be surpassed. Gilt binding, 362 pages.......................$1.50

East Lynne; or, The Earl's Daughter.
Library edition, complete and unabridged. This novel is Mrs. Henry Wood's masterpiece, and stands in the very front ank of all the works of fiction ever written; it has scarcely a riv ' as a brilliant creation of literary genius, and is prominent among the very few works of its class that have stood the test of time, and achieved a lasting reputation. In originality of design, and masterly and dramatic development of the subject, East Lynne stands unrivaled; it will be read and re-read long after the majority of the ephemeral romances of to-day have passed out of existence and been forgotten. A handsome 12mo volume of 598 pages, from new electrotype plates, printed on fine toned paper, and elegantly bound in cloth, in black and gold...$1.50

"Trump's" American Hoyle; or, Gentleman's

Hand-Book of Games. This work contains an exhaustive treatise on Whist, by William Pole, F.R.S., and the rules for playing that game as laid down by the Hon. James Clay. It also contains clear descriptions of all the games played in the United States, with the American rules for playing them; including

Euchre, Bezique, Cribbage, Baccara, All Fours, Loo, Poker, Brag, Piquet, Pedro Sancho, Penuchle. Railroad Euchre. Jack Pots, Ecarté, Boston,

California Jack, Cassino, Chess, Checkers, Backgammon, Billiards, Dominoes, and a hundred other games.

This work is designed as an American authority in all games of skill and chance, and will settle any disputed point. It has been prepared with great care, and is not a re-hash of English games, but a live American book, expressly prepared for American players. THE AMERICAN HOYLE contains 525 pages, is printed on fine white paper, bound in cloth, with extra gilt side and beveled boards, and is profusely illustrated.........$2.00

Spayth's American Draught Player; or, The

Theory and Practice of the Scientific Game of Checkers. Simplified and Illustrated with Practical Diagrams. Containing upwards of 1,700 Games and Positions. By Henry Spayth. Fifth edition, with over two hundred Corrections and Im-

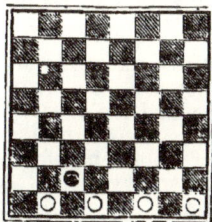

provements. Containing: The Standard Laws of the Game— Full Instructions—Draught Board Numbered—Names of the Games and how formed—The "Theory of the Move and its [...] practically explained and illustrated with Diagrams— [...] or Draught Clubs—New Systems of [...] Signs to the Variations [...] of Draught [...] on Publications chronological [...] arranged. **Boun[d]** [...], gilt side and back.......... [...]

Sut Lovingood. Yarns spun by "A Nat'ral Born Durn'd Fool." Warped and Wove for Public Wear by George W. Harris. Illustrated with eight fine full page engravings,

from designs by Howard. It would be difficult, we think, to cram a larger amount of pungent humor into 300 pages than will be found in this really funny book. The Preface and Dedication are models of sly simplicity, and the 24 Sketches which follow are among the best specimens of broad burlesque to which the genius of the ludicrous, for which the Southwest is so distinguished, has yet given birth. Cloth, gilt edges.........$1.50

How to Conduct a Debate. A Series of
Complete Debates,
Outlines of Debates, and
Questions for Discussion.

In the complete debates, the questions for discussion are defined, the debate formally opened, an array of brilliant arguments adduced on either side, and the debate closed according to parliamentary usages. The second part consists of quest debate, with heads of arguments, for and against, in condensed form for the speaker to enlarge upon to suit his own fancy. In addition

A Treatise on Debatable Questions.

The authorities to be referred to for information are given at the end of every debate. By Frederic Rowton.

222 pages, 1 . . . . .50 cts.
Cloth .75 cts.

LBD 78

www.ingramcontent.com/pod-product-compliance
Lightning Source LLC
Chambersburg PA
CBHW030834270326
41928CB00007B/1046